T0311467

Cambridge Elements ☰

Elements in Psychology and Culture
edited by
Kenneth D. Keith
University of San Diego

PSYCHOLOGY'S WEIRD PROBLEMS

Guilherme Sanches de Oliveira
Technical University of Berlin
Edward Baggs
University of Southern Denmark

CAMBRIDGE
UNIVERSITY PRESS

Shaftesbury Road, Cambridge CB2 8EA, United Kingdom

One Liberty Plaza, 20th Floor, New York, NY 10006, USA

477 Williamstown Road, Port Melbourne, VIC 3207, Australia

314–321, 3rd Floor, Plot 3, Splendor Forum, Jasola District Centre,
New Delhi – 110025, India

103 Penang Road, #05–06/07, Visioncrest Commercial, Singapore 238467

Cambridge University Press is part of Cambridge University Press & Assessment,
a department of the University of Cambridge.

We share the University's mission to contribute to society through the pursuit of
education, learning and research at the highest international levels of excellence.

www.cambridge.org
Information on this title: www.cambridge.org/9781009303514

DOI: 10.1017/9781009303538

First published 2023

A catalogue record for this publication is available from the British Library.

ISBN 978-1-009-30351-4 Paperback
ISSN 2515-3986 (online)
ISSN 2515-3943 (print)

Cambridge University Press & Assessment has no responsibility for the persistence
or accuracy of URLs for external or third-party internet websites referred to in this
publication and does not guarantee that any content on such websites is, or will
remain, accurate or appropriate.

Psychology's WEIRD Problems

Elements in Psychology and Culture

DOI: 10.1017/9781009303538
First published online: May 2023

Guilherme Sanches de Oliveira
Technical University of Berlin

Edward Baggs
University of Southern Denmark

Author for correspondence: Guilherme Sanches de Oliveira,
gui.cogsci@gmail.com

Abstract: Psychology has a WEIRD problem. It is overly reliant on participants from Western, Educated, Industrialized, Rich, and Democratic societies. Over the last decade this problem has come to be widely acknowledged, yet there has been little progress toward making psychology more diverse. This Element proposes that the lack of progress can be explained by the fact that the original WEIRD critique was too narrow in scope. Rather than a single problem of a lack of diversity among research participants, there are at least four overlapping problems. Psychology is WEIRD not only in terms of who makes up its participant pool, but also in terms of its theoretical commitments, methodological assumptions, and institutional structures. Psychology as currently constituted is a fundamentally WEIRD enterprise. Coming to terms with this is necessary if we wish to make psychology relevant for all humanity. This title is also available as Open Access on Cambridge Core.

Keywords: WEIRD psychology, theory and methods, institutional structures and incentives, cross-cultural research, diversity

ISBNs: 9781009303514 (PB), 9781009303538 (OC)
ISSNs: 2515-3986 (online), 2515-3943 (print)

Contents

1 Introduction

In 2010, Joseph Henrich, Steven Heine, and Ara Norenzayan argued that experimental psychology has a problem: it is too reliant on "WEIRD" participants (Henrich, Heine, and Norenzayan, 2010). The acronym denotes that the typical participant in a psychology experiment comes from a background that is Western, Educated, Industrialized, Rich, and Democratic.

Henrich and colleagues were not making a novel observation in pointing out that the behavioral sciences rely heavily on a narrow group of people who routinely serve as participants in experiments. Psychologists had already been joking among themselves for decades about how experimental psychology is really the study of the behavior of college students (Sears, 1986; Smart, 1966). Henrich and colleagues argued, however, that the typical college student is weird in another sense, in addition to the sense denoted by the acronym. The authors claimed that Western college students are also weird in the sense of being unusual. Western college students, they contended, tend to be outliers in terms of their performance on various behavioral tasks. When asked to complete some task in the laboratory, college students tend to perform in ways that make them atypical when compared to noncollege or non-Western humans.

This is a problem because psychologists often assume that what they are really studying when they run experiments in their labs is the behavior and thinking processes of humans in general. However, if, in running these experiments, psychologists are relying on college student participants, and if college students are not representative of humans in general, then a great deal of the published research output of experimental psychology – and that of other behavioral sciences such as behavioral economics – suddenly comes under question.

Henrich and colleagues' argument has received a great deal of attention. However, it is less clear to what extent psychologists have actually changed how they collect their data in response to it. As we will see, in terms of who makes up the experimental participant pool, arguably not much has changed in the decade-and-a-bit since Henrich and colleagues published their paper. The behavioral sciences are still heavily reliant on college student participants (although psychologists' increasing use of online data collection methods has changed this somewhat).

This is not to say that psychologists have been doing nothing, however. In fact, in the past decade or so, psychologists have been quite busy dealing with crises in their field. Coincidentally, Henrich and colleagues' paper came along at about the same time as another crisis was breaking: the crisis of replicability.

1.1 Psychology's Decade of Crisis

The 2010s have been described as a "decade of crisis" for psychology (Nosek et al., 2022). There have been multiple, overlapping crises, but the big one has been a crisis of replicability. The replicability crisis materialized after psychologists began to worry about the possibility, first identified in the biomedical context (Ioannidis, 2005), that many of the published findings in the scientific literature may simply not be true.

The critical year for psychology's replicability crisis was 2011 (Earp and Trafimow, 2015; Makel, Plucker, and Hegarty, 2012; Shrout and Rodgers, 2018). Around this time, a number of high-profile failed replications appeared, as well as several cases of outright scientific misconduct, in which individual psychologists were accused of fabricating data (Pashler and Wagenmakers, 2012; Yong, 2012). Meanwhile, a growing number of psychologists were expressing dissatisfaction with the incentive structures in place for publishing papers in scientific journals (Simmons, Nelson, and Simonsohn, 2011). Journals prioritized the publication of studies with statistically significant results, and studies using novel methodologies. Such a publication landscape creates incentives for individual researchers to engage in questionable research practices. In particular, an incentive arose for researchers to engage in so-called p-hacking – the unscrupulous manipulation of an experiment's design and data in the deliberate pursuit of results that fall below the numerical value that is conventionally considered "statistically significant" – that is, $p < .05$ (Cohen, 1994). Methods of hacking the p-value include formulating a hypothesis after the results are known (HARKing) or continuing to collect data from new participants until a statistically significant sample has been reached and then stopping the collection of data at that point (Simmons et al., 2011).

These issues of skewed incentives are difficult, systemic problems. They have not all been solved yet, but there has been some progress. On the one hand, much effort has been put into trying to accurately assess the scale of the problem, leading to the conclusion that low replicability may not affect all psychological subdisciplines to the same degree (see, e.g., Schimmack, 2020; Tackett et al., 2019; Tackett et al., 2017). On the other hand, even in the subdisciplines most affected, recent changes seem to have brought about improved research practices (Nosek et al., 2022). A number of large-scale replication efforts have been conducted across research consortia made up of multiple labs (Open Science Collaboration, 2015; see also, e.g., Klein et al., 2014). The most high-profile of these saw researchers attempting to replicate 100 studies published in three leading psychology journals (Open Science Collaboration, 2015). Whereas 97 of the original 100 studies presented statistically significant results, only 36 of the replication attempts succeeded in reproducing significant results in the same direction as the original.

At the same time, journal editors and researchers have attempted to reconfigure the incentive structures so that these structures are consistent with the way that psychological science thinks of itself, namely as a dispassionate search for truth. One visible change has been the introduction of badges, which are awarded to published papers if the authors have preregistered their hypotheses before collecting the data, and if they have made their data and research materials openly available for their peers to examine (Kidwell et al., 2016). Institutional structures have been established to support the carrying out of open science, notably the tools provided by the Center for Open Science, which allow researchers to upload data, materials, and draft manuscripts, with the option to make these resources publicly available.

1.2 Four WEIRD Problems

Psychologists, then, have moved quickly to address the crisis of replicability in their field – a crisis that seemed to threaten the legitimacy of much of experimental psychology. In terms of addressing the problem of overreliance on college student participants, however, progress has been less clear. In an editorial written to mark the tenth anniversary of Henrich and colleagues' (2010) original WEIRD paper, it is noted that, in terms of the diversity of participants used by psychology researchers in general, "the needle hasn't moved" in the intervening ten years (Apicella, Norenzayan, and Henrich, 2020). The authors of this editorial write: "Most publications still rely mostly or entirely on WEIRD samples, and perhaps more concerning, most still fail to acknowledge the potential existence of population-level variation or even defend the generalization of their WEIRD findings to the species" (Apicella et al., 2020).

Perhaps, given the multiple crises that psychologists have been dealing with for the past decade, it is not surprising that not much has been done to address the issue of the WEIRDness of psychology's participants. On the face of it, it would seem reasonable to say that ensuring the replicability of the existing research methods must take precedence. After all, countering the WEIRD bias will require researchers to run large-scale, multisite studies, using participants from different places around the world. However, what sense is there in running the same study at multiple sites around the world if researchers in a single laboratory cannot even reliably elicit the same pattern of behavior across two separate studies using students readily available locally? The temptation is to tell oneself something like the following. "Sure, it would be nice to recruit a more diverse participant sample. We will get around to it soon! We will get around to it right after we are done fixing all these replicability problems."

We believe that this strategy would be short-sighted. In the pages that follow, we will present the case that addressing the WEIRDness of psychological science is not a problem that we can put off dealing with until after we have put out all the other fires. On the contrary, the WEIRDness of psychology is one of the things that started those other fires in the first place.

The key to seeing why the WEIRD issue is so central is to notice that what is often presented as a single problem – the "WEIRD problem" – is in fact a collection of related theoretical, methodological, and practical assumptions and limitations (Hruschka et al., 2018). We suggest that there is not one single WEIRD problem. There are at least four. Existing discussion of WEIRD issues has often conflated these. The four problems are as follows.

- *The problem of WEIRD participants*. This is the classic problem, as presented by Henrich and colleagues (2010), of a lack of diversity among research participants. It is a real problem with a long history of being discussed by psychologists. This problem is illustrated in Figure 1.

Besides this already widely acknowledged problem of lack of diversity when it comes to experimental sampling, we identify three additional WEIRD problems attending contemporary psychological science.

- *The problem of WEIRD theory*. Here, we move on to assumptions that are made by researchers themselves, who, also being largely educated in the Western intellectual tradition, bring to the study of psychological science a set of preconceptions about what that science should look like. We will focus on two common assumptions: first, the assumption that psychological explanation should be in terms of processes internal to the individual, and, second, the assumption that the findings of psychological science should in principle be universal, meaning that psychology's findings should be valid for all humans. Both of these assumptions are questionable, and we will discuss some possible advantages of rejecting them.
- *The problem of WEIRD methods*. The next problem concerns the methods that are employed in order to generate experimental psychology's empirical data. Much of existing experimental psychology, as carried out on Western college campuses, takes fundamentally the form of school testing. The researcher sets problems for the participant, who dutifully solves those problems. However, if we look further afield, at cognitive and behavioral research that is conducted outside the laboratory, including work by anthropologists, we notice that the school testing model is not the only possible model. Other research methodologies, for instance, involve observing people

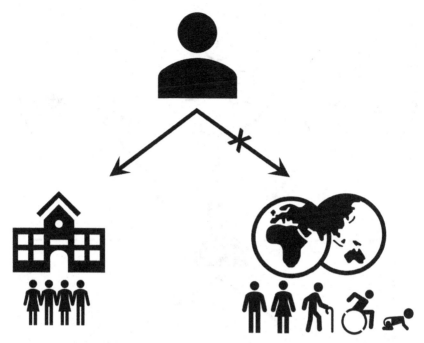

Figure 1 The problem of WEIRD participants is the classic problem that has received most of the attention in the literature following Henrich and colleagues' influential 2010 paper: researchers (top) have been overly reliant on relatively homogeneous samples – predominantly college students in North America and Europe (bottom left) – while neglecting people of different ages, occupations, and backgrounds (linguistic, ethnic, cultural, socioeconomic, political, etc.) in the rest of the world (bottom right).

as they solve problems that they have voluntarily selected for themselves, not artificial problems that have been imposed on them by a teacher–researcher. Studying real behavior in the wild requires a more diverse and open methodological approach than is offered by laboratory-bound experimental psychology.

- *The problem of WEIRD institutions.* The last problem is in some ways the most fundamental. It concerns the organizational structures that support psychological science, as well as the resources used to conduct it and the outputs that document its findings. All of these are necessary features of psychological science as it exists. They are also Western-centric through and through, and may need to be adjusted if psychology is to become capable of supporting a broader and more diverse set of research practices than it has traditionally made use of.

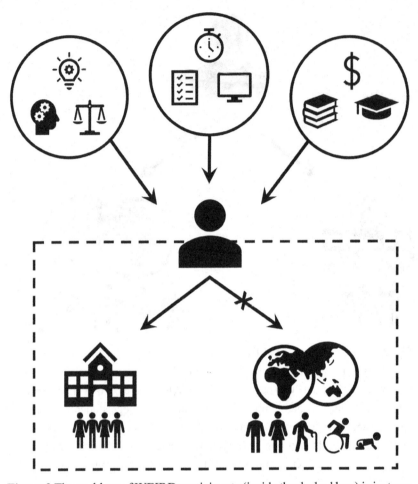

Figure 2 The problem of WEIRD participants (inside the dashed box) is just one of psychology's WEIRD problems. Regardless of who the participants are and where they are from, further problems attending contemporary psychological science include the fact that scientists often take for granted WEIRD theoretical assumptions (top left) and adopt WEIRD methods (top middle) to conduct research that is shaped by WEIRD institutional structures from beginning to end (top right). Solving one WEIRD problem cannot, on its own, automatically solve all of the other ones.

These three additional WEIRD problems are illustrated in Figure 2, which also indicates how they relate to the more well-known sampling problem.

In the rest of this Element, we devote a section to each of these problems. We conclude with a final section looking ahead to a future psychological science that is less constrained by its present WEIRD limitations.

2 WEIRD Participants

In the life sciences, it is common for researchers to make use of model organisms. A model organism is a convenient, readily available animal that scientists can handle in the laboratory, and that can be used in day-to-day research. In genetics, an important model organism is the nematode worm *C. elegans*. This was the first multicellular organism for which scientists developed a map of its entire genome. In medical research, a commonly used model organism is the laboratory mouse. In practical terms, it is easier to test potential medical interventions on mice than it is to test directly on humans, the eventual beneficiaries of the research.

In experimental psychology, the most convenient model organism has traditionally been the college psychology major. In common with the other model organisms just mentioned, college students are a readily available and cheap resource. College students tend to be easy to find, and they often do not have to be paid to participate in research but will participate for course credit.

Relying on college students as the main source of research participants does, however, have potential disadvantages. One worry is that the student population is likely to be unrepresentative of humanity as a whole. College students tend to come from a narrow slice of the overall population. They tend to be in their late teens or early twenties. They tend to be relatively successful academically (they are successful enough academically that they were able to enroll in a university). They also tend to be from the kind of social background that college students come from. In North America, this tends to mean that they are relatively affluent and disproportionately middle class and white (Graham, 1992; Sears, 1986).

If, as an experimental psychologist, you are routinely drawing on this population of college students as participants for your experiments, then how can you know that your experiments are telling you anything useful about humans in general? How can you be sure that you are not inadvertently obtaining data that are only really meaningful or informative about college students?

Concerns about overreliance on college student participants can be traced back to the early decades of social psychology research in the first half of the twentieth century. In 1946, one researcher, working on methodological issues in attitude and opinion research, wrote:

> The existing science of human behavior is largely the science of the behavior of [college] sophomores. Too much research effort is expended on college students with subsequent waste of journal space devoted to speculation concerning whether the findings hold for mankind in general. There may be research problems in the attitude and opinion field which can be profitably

attacked on the local campus, but it is the responsibility of the proponent of such research to show how the project can lead to generalizations which are not so restricted as to be meaningless. (McNemar, 1946, p. 333)

Twenty years later, another researcher concluded that "the male college student has become the 'white rat' of human experimentation and . . . a broadening of the bases for selecting subjects for experiments is in order" (Smart, 1966).

2.1 Psychology's Shallow Participant Pool

These quotations indicate that psychologists have sometimes caricatured their own field as heavily reliant on college student participants. Is it really the case, however, that the participant pool in experimental psychology is so narrow? Perhaps these psychologists merely held a biased view of what their colleagues were doing. One way to find out is to systematically search through the published articles that appear in specialist psychology journals and to count up how many of the studies use college students as participants. As it happens, psychology researchers have been doing this kind of counting exercise since at least the early 1960s, particularly in the field of social psychology.

In 1961, one researcher surveyed the papers published in a leading social psychology journal in the final year of each of the two preceding decades, 1949 and 1959. Comparing the articles published in these two years, he found a trend for increased reliance on college students as participants. The number of studies using college student samples rose from 20% in 1949 to 49% in 1959. In addition, the researcher noted a narrowing of methodologies employed for the collection and analysis of data. Social psychology was not only becoming more dependent on college student participants, it was also becoming more laboratory-based and more reliant on statistical analysis. The researcher wrote wryly: "An extrapolation of the preceding documented trends would indicate that within a few years the number of published articles in the *Journal of Abnormal and Social Psychology* should reach an asymptote with all articles reporting experiments on college students using analysis of variance designs" (Christie, 1965, pp. 150–151, as quoted in Higbee and Wells, 1972, p. 963).

These figures suggest that during the 1950s, social psychology was crystallizing into a laboratory-based enterprise. Earlier social psychology research had been more diverse, both in its participant pool and in its methodology. Proportionately, a greater amount of the research done before the 1950s was carried out in field settings such as factories and military training facilities, and it was common for published papers to present case studies rather than controlled experiments (Sears, 1986).

Subsequent analysis extended this kind of systematic survey of published research to later decades, using a broader sample of journals (Higbee and Wells, 1972; Higbee, Lott, and Graves, 1976, Higbee, Millard, and Folkman, 1982; Sears, 1986). In 1969, 61% of the articles published in four leading social psychology journals made use of college student participants. By 1979, in the same four journals, the number had increased to 70% (Higbee et al., 1982). From the 1960s onward, then, a clear majority of social psychology research was based on college student samples. Comparable numbers were found through to the end of the century, not just in social psychology research but also in experimental psychology research more broadly (Gallander Wintre, North, and Sugar, 2001; Peterson, 2001).

A related concern is that social psychology is reliant not merely on college students, but also on English-speaking college students in the United States. An analysis of leading American Psychological Association (APA) journals from 2003 to 2007 found that 68% of participant samples were from the United States, while an additional 14% were from other English-speaking countries and 13% were from non-English-speaking countries in Europe (Arnett, 2008). The rest of the world – including the whole of Asia, Latin America, and Africa – provided only around 5% of the participant samples in the studies surveyed.

Meanwhile, even for research conducted within the United States, some researchers have long expressed concern that potential research populations have been neglected if they are not from a white and middle-class background. This concern applies not only to laboratory-based experimental studies, but also to community-based studies, including work on child development and family environments (Graham, 1992; Parke, 2000).

2.2 The Birth of the WEIRD

In 2010, Henrich and colleagues published their article titled "The Weirdest People in the World?" – in which they coined the WEIRD acronym. Up to this point, as indicated, psychologists had argued for decades over whether it posed a problem for psychology that so many of the field's research findings were the result of experiments conducted on college students in the United States. The concern was that psychology's reliance on college student participants might, in principle, be providing a distorted picture of human psychology. However, little hard evidence existed to show that the use of college student participants in fact did yield a distorted picture of human psychology. It might, after all, be the case that US college students think and behave very much like everyone else. In that case, the overrepresentation of college students within psychology research might not actually pose a problem for the field after all.

Missing was a systematic comparison of college students against noncollege students as participants carrying out the exact same experimental tasks. The main innovation of Henrich and colleagues' 2010 article, other than coining the WEIRD acronym, was that it attempted to do just this. The authors attempted to compare college students against noncollege students in like-for-like task settings and across a range of task types. Based on their survey of the psychological literature, the authors concluded that US college students really are unusual and that they are frequently unrepresentative of human psychology in general. In fact, the authors claimed, college students from the United States systematically tend to perform in ways that make them outliers across a wide variety of tasks. The responses of US college students in experimental task settings put them at extreme ends of the measurement distribution when compared with the broader population.

Henrich and colleagues (2010) present their case in a telescoping series of contrasts. We here briefly summarize their main evidence. The authors cite evidence from multiple areas of psychology, not just social psychology.

The first contrast is between participants from industrialized societies versus participants from small-scale societies. Henrich and colleagues here point to evidence from studies of visual perception, specifically to work purporting to show that people from small-scale traditional societies are less susceptible to certain visual illusions such as the Müller–Lyer illusion, where two lines of identical length are seen as of different lengths depending on which way the arrowheads are pointing. The effect of the illusion has been found to be reduced in participants from small-scale societies, while the effect is strongest for observers from the United States, perhaps because the latter have grown up in environments that contain many "carpentered corners" (Cole, 1996; Segall, Campbell, and Herskovits, 1966; the reader is directed to Henrich and colleagues' article and to the works cited there for details of the exact populations studied). Next, Henrich and colleagues point to earlier work by Henrich and a group of colleagues in which two economic games – the dictator game and the ultimatum game – were administered to participants from either the United States or from a range of small-scale societies. Again, the US participants appear at one extreme end of the response distribution, giving the most "fair" offers (they offer close to 50% of a reward pool) compared to participants from 14 small-scale societies (Henrich et al., 2010). The remaining evidence involves linguistic reasoning. The authors point to work that claims to demonstrate systematic differences in how people from different societies categorize objects. For participants from industrial societies, categorization is based on the broad class of things to which an object belongs – for example, "tree" – but this is not typical of small-scale societies where the basic scale of classification is the species – for example, "maple" or "oak" (Medin and Atran, 2004; Berlin, 1992). Finally, the authors discuss work on linguistic classification of space, pointing out that the egocentric model of describing space in terms of "left" and "right" relative to one's own body is not the only method of classifying space, and many societies use an environment-centered classification scheme instead – for example, classifying space primarily in terms of "north" versus "south." There is a debate over the extent to which such spatial classification schemes affect how we orient to the world around us (Levinson et al., 2002; Li and Gleitman, 2002).

The second of Henrich and colleagues' telescoping series of contrasts examined participants from industrial societies in "the West" (a category in which the authors only explicitly include countries in Northern but not Southern Europe, along with the United States, Canada, Australia, and New Zealand; see their footnote 7) in comparison with participants from non-Western industrial societies. Here, Henrich and colleagues again cite evidence from an economic game, this time the public goods game. When playing this type of game, participants from Western countries, including Switzerland and the United States, are consistently shown to punish free riding, or noncooperative behavior, in other participants. However, in "non-Western" countries (including Russia and Saudi Arabia), participants additionally show a tendency to punish overly generous cooperative behavior, a punishment behavior rarely seen when Western participants play the game (Herrmann, Thoni, and Gachter, 2008). Henrich and colleagues also cite evidence of differences in reasoning styles between Westerners and non-Westerners. For instance, when asked to look at a picture of an object on a background, Westerners spend more time looking at the object while non-Westerners spend more time looking at the background. Based on such evidence, Westerners are said to engage in a style of reasoning dubbed "analytic," while non-Western reasoning is more "holistic" (Norenzayan, Choi, and Peng, 2007). Last, the authors discuss differences in moral reasoning styles between Westerners and non-Westerners. They claim that, whereas Westerners tend to engage in abstract moral reasoning, judging the morality of an action according to principles such as the golden rule, non-Westerners are more likely to judge the morality of an action based on a broader range of factors, such as whether the action threatens social order within the community (Shweder et al., 1997).

The third contrast is between US participants and non-US Westerners. Here the authors acknowledge that they were able to find little direct evidence comparing US and non-US Westerners on the same psychological tasks.

Given this lack of evidence, they instead rely on various social outcomes as evidence that people in the United States are unusually individualistic, even compared to people from other Western countries. They write:

> In contrast to other large Western industrialized societies, the United States had the highest crime rate, the longest working hours, the highest divorce rate, the highest rate of volunteerism, the highest percentage of citizens with a post-secondary education, the highest productivity rate, the highest GDP, the highest poverty rate, and the highest income-inequality rate; and Americans were the least supportive of various governmental interventions. (Henrich et al., 2010, p. 75)

The fourth and final contrast is between US college students and other, noncollege-student US participants. Here the authors point yet again to evidence from economic games. They claim that, when playing the dictator game, US college students are less generous in their offers than are their nonstudent compatriots. The authors also suggest that changes in the content of the typical US education may have had an impact on the reasoning styles of the young research participants of today compared to research participants of earlier generations. They note that IQ test scores in industrialized nations rose by 18 points over half a century, and that this increase was driven by increases in scores on analytic parts of IQ tests (Flynn, 2007). "Given such findings," the authors write, "it seems plausible that Americans of only 50 or 100 years ago were reasoning in ways much more similar to the rest of the non-Western world than Americans of today" (Henrich et al., 2010, p. 78).

The authors conclude that the participants typically used in psychological research – US college students – are unrepresentative and may therefore be "one of the worst subpopulations one could study for generalizing about *Homo sapiens*" (Henrich et al., 2010, p. 79).

2.3 The Rise of the Online Research Participant

Henrich and colleagues' 2010 article has had a huge impact on experimental psychology, at least on the level of discourse. The acronym WEIRD has entered into common usage both within the field and outside it. It is less clear that the paper has, so far, had a substantial impact on how psychologists recruit their participants or carry out their research. A survey of research published in prestigious psychology journals in the years 2014–2018 suggests that the kinds of participants used in psychology experiments are similar to those used a decade earlier (Thalmayer, Toscanelli, and Arnett, 2021). Participant samples in studies published in these years in top APA journals still came predominantly from the United States (62%, down from 68% a decade earlier), other English-speaking countries (14%, unchanged), and other European countries (17%, up from 13%).

There has, however, been one notable change in the profile of research participants in recent years. This change has been caused by the rise of online microwork platforms, in particular by Amazon's launch of its Mechanical Turk platform. Through Mechanical Turk, experimenters can now easily recruit participants and conduct experiments entirely online, bypassing the traditional college student participant pool. The platform allows researchers to solicit responses to surveys and other tasks. Researchers can specify the number of responses that they require. Once the survey is published on the site, online users can complete it, usually in return for small cash payments (Buhrmester, Kwang, and Gosling, 2011).

The rise of the use of online platforms in experimental psychology research has been rapid. Amazon launched Mechanical Turk in 2005. Ten years later, research papers were routinely being published using samples from Mechanical Turk, including in top journals such as the *Journal of Personality and Social Psychology* (*JPSP*), the flagship journal of social psychology. In the period from 2014 to 2018, 35% of studies published in *JPSP* drew their participant samples from Mechanical Turk alone, while an additional 2% of samples were drawn from rival online platforms (Thalmayer et al., 2021). Most researchers in social psychology expect that, in the coming years, the field will increasingly rely on online platforms for conducting experiments (Goodman and Wright, 2022). At the same time, researchers in different subdisciplines and fields outside psychology have also emphasized the many potential ethical challenges arising from this shift (e.g., Fort, Adda, and Cohen, 2011; Gleibs and Albayrak-Aydemir, 2022; Litman and Robinson, 2020; Moss et al., 2020a; Shank, 2016; Williamson, 2016).

The use of online platforms has implications for the kinds of participants psychologists can recruit. These online platforms can be accessed by anyone on the Internet, and they therefore potentially offer a more diverse sample than the traditional college participant pool. In practice, however, the type of people who routinely carry out work tasks on Mechanical Turk still represent a narrow sample of the entire human population. Workers come predominantly from the United States and India, and, compared to the general population, they are younger, more educated, relatively underemployed, less religious, and more liberal (Paolacci and Chandler, 2014). The demographic profile of Mechanical Turk workers has reportedly remained stable over time (Moss et al., 2020b), although with some fluctuations. For example, at the start of the Covid-19 pandemic, some researchers reported an increase in new users (Arechar and Rand, 2021).

In principle, the use of online platforms could allow experimental psychologists to diversify their participant sample well beyond the traditional pool of college sophomores. Psychologists should, however, be wary of the possibility that, by relying on platforms such as Mechanical Turk, they are in fact replacing one narrow pool of college student participants with a different, but equally narrow group of people engaged in online gig work.

2.4 Addressing the WEIRD Participants Problem

It would seem there is still much work to be done if psychology and the behavioral sciences are to address the WEIRD participants problem. The obvious solution to the problem is that psychologists should simply recruit research participants from a more diverse variety of backgrounds, ideally from both rural and urban settings, and across a variety of continents and linguistic populations. This solution, however, faces substantial practical challenges. A more modest solution is that researchers should reform their reporting standards. For instance, researchers could be more transparent about the limitations of their existing sampling methods, and they could be more clear about how generalizable they expect their findings to be.

Mostafa Salari Rad and colleagues (2018) offer a series of recommendations along these more modest lines. They divide their recommendations into two sets, one for authors and one for editors and reviewers. For authors, they recommend:

- Required reporting of sample characteristics, including not only participants' gender (which is already routinely reported) but also age, socioeconomic status, ethnicity, religion, and nationality.
- Explicitly tying findings to the sampled population – for example, avoiding overly broad statements such as "knitting increases attractiveness" in favor of more precise statements such as "knitting increases attractiveness according to Mechanical Turk participants in the United States."
- Justifying the choice of the sampled population in the same way authors currently justify the sample size.
- Discussing whether the finding can be generalized to other populations beyond the sample.
- Performing statistical analyses on the data to check for effects of participants' cultural background, in the same way studies often test for gender effects.

Salari Rad and colleagues (2018) offer three recommendations for reviewers and editors:

- Prioritize non-WEIRD samples as novel and important and therefore as more worthy of publication.
- Add diversity badges to published papers to incentivize more diverse sampling (similar to the aforementioned badges incentivizing open science).

- Set journal-wide targets for diversity of samples. Salari Rad and colleagues (2018) suggest that journals such as *Psychological Science* should aim for at least 50% of their published papers to include a non-WEIRD sample.

This set of recommendations is similar to recommendations offered by others, including Henrich and colleagues (2010) and Arnett (2008). See also the updated set of recommendations in Thalmayer, Toscanelli and Arnett (2021).

These recommendations are sensible, and we think psychology would be improved if they were implemented, particularly the recommendation about discussing the generalizability of findings (see also Simons, Shoda, and Lindsay, 2017). These recommendations are also clearly limited in scope, however. For one, they do not explicitly address the need for changes in incentive structures, beyond the superficial implementation of badges. The recommendations say nothing of the need for changes in training and mentoring practices now so future generations of scientists are better positioned to act differently both as researchers–authors and as editors–reviewers. Moreover, these recommendations are still predominantly inward looking and Western-centric: they focus on how individual scientists from WEIRD contexts can make their own research more diverse, but without acknowledging the need to make the discipline as a whole more diverse, including by supporting researchers from low-income, non-WEIRD contexts. These neglected aspects of the current discussion are central to what we will explore in the upcoming sections.

For us, the interesting question is the following. If researchers implemented all of these recommendations, would it lead to a psychology that more accurately represents the whole of humanity? Will we end up with a science of *Homo sapiens* if we simply sample a more representative set of research participants, beyond US college students and underpaid online gig workers?

In the rest of this Element, we will argue that merely sampling a more diverse population will not be enough to give us a comprehensive science of humanity. This is because the WEIRD participants problem is only one of psychology's WEIRD problems. The other problems go deeper, and concern psychology's underlying theories and methods, as well as the institutions within which psychology is conducted.

3 WEIRD Theory

Here is a thought experiment. Imagine that psychologists could study all of the people in the entire world. This is unrealistic, of course. When running our experiments, we do not have the financial and technical resources to recruit billions of participants. Not only that, but processing so much data would be impractical. Let us bracket considerations like these. Assume for the sake of argument that these limitations no longer hold and that psychologists can feasibly run their studies and collect data from every single human being currently alive. What would this mean for psychological science?

One thing we can be certain of is that the *problem of WEIRD participants* examined in the previous section would immediately disappear. If suddenly it was possible to obtain data from every person alive – let us call this "total sampling" – then psychology would no longer have a problem of WEIRD participants. The data collected would necessarily be perfectly representative of humans in general, having a one-to-one correspondence to the total human population.

In such a scenario, would there be anything left about psychological science that would make it problematically WEIRD? We think so – that is what this Element is about. In this section, we focus on a *theoretical* problem attending psychological science that even this hypothetical solution to the problem of WEIRD participants via total sampling would leave unaddressed. The problem in question is the way in which virtually all of psychological science is shaped by the WEIRD theoretical assumptions of *individualism* and *universalism*.

3.1 Individualism and Universalism in Psychological Explanation

In presenting what we called the "problem of WEIRD participants," we saw how the relevant literature is rife with discussions of the differences between WEIRD and non-WEIRD people, especially when it comes to their values, beliefs, and attitudes toward themselves and others.

On the one hand, people from WEIRD societies are described as more individualistic, for instance, valuing their autonomy and personal goals and opinions more highly than they value the interests of the group(s) they belong to. This contrast with the collectivism more common among non-WEIRD people is sometimes described as the prevalence of an independent orientation rather than an *inter*dependent one, and it is supported by empirical findings, such as from economic games (Henrich, 2020; Henrich et al., 2010).

On the other hand, besides being more individualistic, WEIRD people are also described as more often holding a *universalist* outlook. Given our tendency to see individuals as more important than the groups they form, it is also common in WEIRD culture to see individuals as on equal footing *with one another*, independently of the specific groups to which they happen to belong. Cross-cultural empirical research suggests this is very different from the "parochialism" more often found in non-WEIRD societies, where it is more common and even expected that people will treat more favorably those who belong to their own group (e.g., family, clan, tribe, or ethnic or linguistic group) compared to the way they treat out-group individuals (Bernhard, Fischbacher, and Fehr, 2006; Choi and Bowles, 2007; Henrich, 2015, 2020; Hruschka and Henrich, 2013; Lang et al., 2019; Norenzayan et al., 2016).

Our interest here is in a slightly different sense of individualism and universalism. In the usual sense just seen, individualism and universalism correspond to beliefs, values, and attitudes that can be objects of psychological investigation: in particular, they designate psychological features commonly thought to mark WEIRD people as psychologically unusual and unrepresentative of humans more generally – that is, they illustrate the psychological WEIRDness of the typical research participants. In contrast, our goal here is to explore individualism and universalism understood not as psychological traits and objects of psychological investigation, but rather as theoretical and methodological assumptions that shape investigation in psychological science. We will refer to these as "scientific" commitments to emphasize our focus on what *psychologists* think and do. That is, in contrast with the individualism and universalism that psychologists often find in WEIRD participants, we focus on the individualism and universalism at play in how (typically WEIRD) psychologists construe psychology's object of investigation, shaping how they understand and study mind and behavior, regardless of whose – whether of WEIRD or non-WEIRD participants.

3.2 Scientific Individualism

Psychology is the science of mind and behavior. This formulation is found in many undergraduate psychology textbooks, and is often seen as reflecting a historical compromise between competing approaches that have been dominant at different points in time. A common version of the story describes a pendulum swinging between mind and behavior as the focus of research, from the introspectionist, subjectivist roots of psychology (with its emphasis on mind), the half century or so of behaviorist dominance (with its exclusive focus on behavior to the detriment of mind), with the current cognitivist paradigm falling somewhere in the middle and including aspects of both internal mental processes and observable behavior.

This narrative is superficial, at best, and alternative historical accounts emphasize different tensions, especially external ones (between psychology and other disciplines and professions), as shaping psychological science's identity (see, e.g, Danziger, 1990, 1997). Details of this history fall outside the scope of this Element, however. Particularly relevant for us at this point is to see how dominant conceptions of the object of study in psychological science – however they came about – reflect a commitment to individualist and universalist scientific assumptions.

The individualism characteristic of psychological theorizing is evident in how, understood as the science of mind and behavior, psychology is also taken to be a science of individuals – and not, for instance, a science of communities or other collective structures and groups. Psychological phenomena – that is, the phenomena that psychological science studies – are phenomena at the level of individual people, and even when we talk about groups, that is usually in terms of an aggregation of individual attitudes, intentions, beliefs, and so on. In common and currently dominant "internalist" versions, individualism motivates construing "human action as the product of *individual* mental processes" (Harré, 1984, p. 8, emphasis added). Philosopher Charles Taylor describes this as corresponding to the widely assumed opposition between what is inside the individual and what is outside: "We think of our thoughts, ideas, or feelings as being 'within' us, while the objects in the world which these mental states bear on are 'without.' Or else we think of our capacities or potentialities as 'inner,' awaiting the development which will manifest them or realize them in the public world" (Taylor, 1989, p. 111). Much the same point applies to trends in psychological science, past and present, which resist the focus on internal states and processes: even while emphasizing overt bodily behavior, it is the behavior of the *individual subject* that is typically considered the proper locus for psychological investigation. Whether implicitly or explicitly, both internalist and "externalist" (e.g., behaviorist) perspectives thus embrace individualism when they accept the opposition "between what belongs [to] the individual and what belongs to a social sphere entirely outside the individual" (Danziger, 1997, p. 4) and, accordingly, see mind and behavior as intrinsically individual.

This individualist way of construing psychological phenomena becomes most evident in discussions about the boundaries between scientific disciplines. Consider, for instance, discussions in the social sciences surrounding the notion of "methodological individualism" in the tradition initiated by Max Weber (1922). Weberian methodological individualism has been described as claiming that "social phenomena must be explained by showing how they result from individual actions, which in turn must be explained through reference to the intentional states that motivate the individual actors" (Heath, 2020). It is interesting that the idea of treating the individual as the locus for sociological explanation subsequently turns into a threatening possibility that sociology would be subsumed by psychology (see, e.g., Webster, 1973): underlying this concern on the part of some sociologists is the idea that *explanation at the level of the individual* can be seen as one and the same as *psychological explanation*. This assumption has been common throughout the history of psychological science: "Locating the object of research within an isolated individual person was of course a basic common feature of all forms of psychological investigation; in fact, this constituted it as psychological, rather than some other kind of investigation" (Danziger, 1990, p. 56).

3.3 Scientific Universalism

The individualist assumption just considered is also intimately tied to the universalism of psychological science. Throughout psychology's history, it has been common, as Danziger describes it, for researchers to interpret experimental observations (typically of single participants), not "as conveying information about an individual-in-a-situation but about an individual in isolation whose characteristics existed independently of any social involvement" (Danziger, 1990, p. 186). The work by Wilhelm Wundt and his followers in Leipzig in the mid-to-late 1800s provides a compelling and relevant example of the connection between universalism and individualism, and in particular, given Wundt's pioneering role in experimental psychology, an illustration of how they (and so many psychologists since) came to see the individual subject:

> Experimental subjects were not studied as individual persons but as examples that displayed certain common human characteristics. That is why the role of subject could be assumed by any member of the research community. They did not represent themselves but their common mental processes. These "elementary" mental processes, as Wundt called them, were assumed to be natural objects that could be studied independently of the whole personality. All that was necessary were the restricted conditions of the laboratory and a certain preparation of the subject. (Danziger, 1990, p. 52)

As Danziger explains, researchers in the Wundtian school believed that a single participant was all it took as evidence: in their view, to use more recent terminology, each additional participant and experimental measurement would be a replication of the initial finding. Moreover, as suggested in the quote just cited, Wundt and his colleagues saw the roles of experimenter and participant as interchangeable, to the point that lab members often took turns serving as experimental participants for one another – this is clear from their publications, which often identified by name both the experimenter and the single participant studied in each case. In support of the interchangeability of roles and the sufficiency of a single measurement was the idea that the regularities of sensation and perception under investigation were basic "biological processes involved in the functioning of [all] normal, mature organisms" (Danziger, 1990, p. 52): while measured in the individual instance, these regularities were general, universal, applying to anyone and everyone.

Undoubtedly, several aspects of psychological theorizing and research methodology have changed since Wundt, even drastically. The combination of individualism and universalism has endured, however. The general description of the combination of individualism and universalism within the Wundtian tradition also applies, for instance, to the laws of conditioning in behaviorist psychology as well as to the algorithms and models of cognitive psychology: in each case, the psychological phenomenon in question manifests itself in an individual instance (that is what makes it psychological), but individual instances are considered illuminating because they are taken to be revelatory of more general, universal patterns, structures, or laws. This assumption is also alluded to, in the long quote by Danziger, in the idea that universal psychological phenomena could be "studied independently of the whole personality." This use of the term "personality" to refer to the totality of an individual's psychological makeup is different from more recent ways in which psychologists study "personality," namely in terms of "traits" (such as openness and extraversion) that individuals possess in different amounts but that are universal, the same for everyone: in this more recent usage, "One abstract trait [differs] qualitatively from other abstract traits, but individuals [are] limited to possessing larger or smaller quantities of identical features" (Danziger, 1990, p. 159).

In sum, individualism amounts to the idea that psychological phenomena – the phenomena of mind and behavior – are ontologically situated at the individual level: they exist as attributes or qualities of individuals, and are properly investigated and explained at this level. Universalism leads to thinking that psychological phenomena at the individual level are particular instances of more general, biological processes and structures. This is a view with a long history. Looking back, Charles Taylor describes this view using the words of sixteenth-century philosopher Michel de Montaigne, for whom "every man beareth the whole stampe of humane condition" (Taylor, 1989, p. 179). In more recent biological terminology, it amounts to a "view of human nature as variations on a species-typical theme" (Barrett, 2020). However, their long history and familiarity do not make the theoretical assumptions of individualism and universalism any more real or scientifically established – and, importantly, they do not make these theoretical assumptions any less WEIRD.

3.4 What Does the Science of Mind and Behavior Study?

As the foregoing discussion suggested, the assumptions of individualism and universalism are not only closely tied to one another, but they are also tightly linked to biological ideas about how individuals relate to species, and about the "psychological" in relation to nature and to culture. Let us return to the definition of psychology we discussed earlier, and let us now ask: what does the science of mind and behavior study? An intuitive individualist and universalist answer is that a science of mind and behavior is (or should be) in the business of understanding the psychological dimension of *universal human nature.*

This view of human nature as the goal of psychological science is common in the literature on the WEIRD problem. As seen in Section 2 ("WEIRD Participants"), in putting forward the label "WEIRD," Henrich and colleagues referred to WEIRD participants as "one of the worst subpopulations one could study for generalizing about *Homo sapiens*" (Henrich et al., 2010, p. 79). The authors also claim, based on their survey of the psychological literature, "that we need to be less cavalier in addressing questions of human nature on the basis of data drawn from this particularly thin, and rather unusual [WEIRD], slice of humanity" (p. 61). Much the same reasoning is found elsewhere. In adopting the label "WEIRD," many other researchers have also expressed a similar perspective on why being exclusively reliant on WEIRD participants is detrimental to psychological science, namely because it hinders our ability to generalize about the human species; it gets in the way of understanding universal human nature. Along these lines, for instance, Salari Rad and colleagues (2018) begin their paper by asserting that "two core goals in psychological science should be to understand human universals and the way in which context and culture produce variability" (p. 11401). They add, "It is impossible to isolate universals without investigating variability" (p. 11401).

Views like these illustrate the widespread commitment among psychologists to the thoroughly individualist and universalist idea that *there is such a thing as a universal human nature* – a common mental core shared by all typically developing individual humans – and that this is what psychology is in pursuit of when it investigates mind and behavior. According to this view, some characteristics of human beings are natural (they originate within universal human nature) while others are cultural (they are learned from or somehow influenced by other individuals). Cultural factors are then thought to explain our psychological WEIRDness, and consequently to explain why WEIRD people have become outliers and unrepresentative of human psychology more generally: cultural factors have made WEIRD people unrepresentative of universal (i.e., biological) human nature.

This perspective is couched in terms that make it sound scientifically unquestionable, but in fact it is not as well supported as it may seem. In particular, this individualist and universalist idea of psychological science as the study of human nature is rooted in biological views that, although long-standing and still influential, have in recent decades come to be challenged. This is the case both in developmental biology and in evolutionary biology, where recent theories reject the idea that culture is a source of variation distinct from "nature."

In the developmental domain, it is common to think that natural factors (genetics) and environmental factors (e.g. culture, or "nurture") are two separate sources of organismal form and that developmental outcomes are the product of their *interaction*. Developmental systems theory rejects this view, proposing that there is no interaction between nature and nurture because the two are not separate in the first place – rather, what is natural is precisely that organisms develop differently due to their different histories, including the social and environmental aspects of that history (see Box 1).

BOX 1 HOW DEVELOPMENTAL SYSTEMS THEORY CHALLENGES "UNIVERSAL HUMAN NATURE"

The traditional "nature–nurture debate" in developmental biology is predicated on the assumption of a strict distinction between traits that are inherited and therefore natural, and traits that are acquired and therefore the product of nurture (see Keller, 2010). Pretty much all biological theorists today are in agreement that the debate is solved because it is a case not of *either/or* but of *both/and*: nature and nurture always interact. Developmental systems theory takes this interactionist reasoning further. Developmental systems theory challenges the notion of two separable, interacting causes that could, in principle, be disentangled. It challenges the fundamental idea that nature and nurture can in fact be treated as separable sources of organismal form.

The key observation is that development is a process that unfolds over time. The organism's genes are always present throughout that process, as is the organism's environment. The two cannot be separated in principle because you can never observe how the organism would have developed under the influence of only the genes in isolation from the environment, or vice versa. Outlining an alternative way of thinking, Susan Oyama (1985/ 2000, p. 39) writes:

> What we are moving toward is a conception of a developmental system, not as the reading off of a preexisting code, but as a complex of interacting influences, some inside the organism's skin, some external to it, and many including its ecological niche in all its spatial and temporal aspects, *many of which are typically passed on in reproduction* either because they are in some way tied to the organism's (or its conspecifics') activities or characteristics or because they are stable features of the general environment.

On this way of thinking, it simply does not make sense to talk of a universal human nature as one source of organismal form among others.

Developmental systems theory emphasizes understanding development in terms of the whole complex system that includes not only the organism's genes and its immediate physical surroundings, but also the other organisms around it.

Two different individual organisms may be very different from one another in many respects, and it is true that we readily identify some individual human characteristics as resulting from a particular cultural upbringing. What is "natural" is precisely the process itself. The developmental process entails that mature organisms differ as a result of the many different aspects of their particular histories. Human nature, on the developmental systems view, is understood as the *outcome* of the developmental process, not as one (biological, natural) source of form that is supposed to already exist at the outset, among others (Oyama, Gray, and Griffiths, 2003; Stotz and Griffiths, 2018). Crucially, *development is not a battle between internal biological starting conditions and externally imposed cultural deviations that push the outcome away from what it would naturally have been.* Although we may for analytic purposes wish to identify different aspects of the system with the labels "nature" and "culture," ultimately these do not amount to ontologically separate forces that exert independent influences: "The biological, the psychological, the social, and the cultural are related not as alternative causes but as levels of analysis" (Oyama 1985/2000, p. 93).

An analogous move has also played out in recent theorizing in evolutionary biology. It can seem intuitive to think that humans have a common biological core ("human nature") that was shaped by natural selection and that, once modern humans emerged, culture entered the picture as the background against or context in which this common core manifests itself, with particular instances varying depending on the different conditions in place. Niche construction theory challenges this perspective by emphasizing the ways in which organismal activity (in the case of humans as well as other species) is not just the product of evolution but also a key contributor to the evolutionary process itself, precluding strict separations between the natural and the agential (e.g., culture) as sources of form (see Box 2).

Crucial for our argument is that recent and increasingly popular views in biological science such as these speak against the common assumption of there being such a thing as a universal human nature in any scientifically intelligible sense. According to these approaches, it does not make sense to posit a universal essence of the human species that already exists as a kind

Box 2 How Niche Construction Theory Challenges "Universal Human Nature"

A simplistic understanding of evolution by natural selection has it that environmental conditions exert pressure on individual members of a species and that this leads, at the population level and over multiple generations (rather than for an individual within its life span), to an increase in survival-enhancing traits and a decrease in traits that are not well suited to those environmental conditions. This is a simplistic view of evolution because it views organisms as passively acted upon by selection pressures, but neglects their role as active agents that selectively bring about conditions favorable to their own continued survival (Lewontin, 1983). Niche construction theory is an example of a recent approach that challenges this simplistic view of evolution. In reality, organisms of all sorts transform their environment by creating and maintaining structures that make the environment better suited to their needs and by changing aspects that are harmful, or alternatively by moving to a different, more hospitable environment. In short, organisms construct their niche. From this observation, niche construction theory proposes that organisms cannot be merely passive recipients of selection pressure, but their niche construction activity constitutes "reciprocal causal processes that act alongside natural selection during the evolution of traits" (Laland and Brown, 2018, p. 130; see also, e.g., Laland, Matthews, and Feldman, 2016; Odling-Smee 1988; Odling-Smee et al., 2013).

Niche construction theory further complicates the idea of the organism as the result of separate sources of form, originating partly in universal human nature, partly in culture. If niche construction theory is correct, then we are forced to recognize that among the influences at play during the developmental process are not only genetic and cultural influences, but also the influence of the organism's environment, which itself is structured partly by the activities of previous generations, and also partly by the organism's own actions (Baggs, Raja, and Anderson, 2019). That is, we must count ourselves and our own past actions as among the influential factors leading to our own present form (Lewontin, 2001). Among other things, this requires a theory of learning in development that again does not conceive learning and maturation as separate sources of form, but recognizes that they are inseparably part of the same process: learning is inherently situated, inherently social, and the learner plays an active role throughout (Adolph, 2019; Baggs, Raja, and Anderson, 2020; Rogoff, 1990).

of blueprint at the outset of individual organismal development. The blueprint metaphor obscures the fact that the process itself constructs the organism. Furthermore, the fact of constructive variability at the spatiotemporal scale of development means that there cannot be an essence that varies through evolution but that all humans at a given point in evolutionary time *universally* share in by nature. On the contrary, if anything applies universally to all human beings, it is the fact that we differ from each other in many ways because our developmental trajectories differ from one another in many ways, and this is a fact of culture as much as of nature because in the end the two are not distinct.

This being the case, psychology cannot be after "universal human nature" because that is not a thing in the first place. Or, to put this point more modestly, the assumption that this is what psychological science is after cannot be embraced and promoted as unquestionable scientific fact. On the contrary, prominent theories in biology cast doubt on the soundness of this assumption, and they give us reason to be wary of notions of a universal psychological core or standard that is manifested, at the individual level, in culturally variable ways. Taking seriously these developments in biological science motivates humbly reconsidering how we as researchers construe psychological phenomena in relation to individuals and species, as well as in relation to biology and culture. Merely appealing to science or scientific-sounding terminology is not enough to justify our culture-bound (i.e., WEIRD) individualist and universalist assumptions.

3.5 The Theoretical WEIRDness of Psychological Science

Individualism and universalism, we have seen, are not just values, beliefs, and attitudes that are prevalent among WEIRD people in comparison to their non-WEIRD counterparts: they also amount to theoretical commitments that psychologists widely share and that have shaped psychological science from the start, informing even how researchers understand psychology's object of study. It is important to realize that individualism and universalism are interconnected, and historical explanations for why WEIRD people have become individualists and universalists also explain (at least in part) why the same WEIRD people, in developing a science of mind and behavior, have tended to make it an individualist and universalist science. To quote Danziger once more, a great danger for psychological science is "that its historically contingent and culturally parochial categories will be mistaken for universal principles having eternal validity" (Danziger, 1997, p. 22). The assumptions of individualism and universalism are so prevalent in the scientific training available in WEIRD countries that, to us WEIRD researchers, they can seem like unquestionable facts about humans.

They are, however, historically contingent conceptions that only seem so compelling and undeniable to us because they are *our* assumptions.

Individualism and universalism are familiar to the point of being transparent to us: they inform how we in the West see the world, but they are typically not themselves noticed and acknowledged. Crucially, however, the problem is not just that individualism and universalism are historically contingent aspects of Western culture – things that are historically contingent can still be good and useful for some purposes. The problem is that even the aura of scientific legitimacy these assumptions enjoy is questionable. As we have seen, individualism and universalism are grounded in biological ideas that recent research in developmental and evolutionary biology shows to be problematic. This means that we cannot talk about what is "natural" as opposed to what is "cultural" in "mind" and "behavior" and pretend we are dealing with natural kinds, as if these were scientifically solid categories that are ahistorical, culturally neutral, and universal. Moreover, given how the biological theories reviewed earlier motivate questioning common notions of "universal human nature," it follows that the problem of WEIRD participants cannot be that our biased sampling gets in the way of understanding universal human nature: if these biological theories are right, then universal human nature is nowhere to be found anyway.

We began this section proposing a hypothetical scenario of total sampling, and we asked: if psychologists could study all of the people in the world, thereby solving the problem of WEIRD participants, would there still be anything problematically WEIRD about psychological science? The preceding discussion should make clear at least part of why our answer is yes: even if researchers in rich, Western countries corrected this bias toward WEIRD participants and sampled much more widely, the work would still be informed by WEIRD individualist and universalist assumptions about the phenomena under investigation. Another way to see this is by considering a different hypothetical scenario: if psychological science had not emerged in WEIRD societies, would it look basically the same, with the same ideas about what is psychological or not, making the same assumptions concerning mind and behavior and understanding them in individualist and universalist terms? It seems doubtful, and in fact many different non-Western traditions (philosophical, religious, spiritual, and so on) operate with psychological concepts and categories that differ widely from those at play in WEIRD psychological science.

The theoretical WEIRDness of psychological science has important methodological implications, which we will consider next. For now, before leaving this more purely theoretical terrain, we want to offer an illustration of just how pervasive and deeply rooted the theoretical assumptions of individualism and universalism are. Earlier we saw, based on cross-cultural empirical research, how individualist and universalist values, beliefs, and attitudes are more prevalent among WEIRD individuals. Is this finding itself free from WEIRD theoretical preconceptions, though?

Consider a finding that Henrich (2020) discusses concerning the "endowment effect" from behavioral economics – that is, the tendency for individuals to favor an item that they already own over an item of ostensibly equivalent value. In classic studies, using WEIRD participants, the participants are given an item – for example, a mug – which they are told is theirs to keep. The participants are then presented with the opportunity to trade that item for a different item of equivalent value – for example, a mug with a different design. WEIRD participants show a preference to keep the first mug (Kahnemam, Knetsch, and Thaler, 1990). WEIRD participants, that is, exhibit an endowment effect. Henrich (2020) discusses a study that attempted to identify the endowment effect in non-WEIRD participants. The study in question involved two groups of participants from two different populations of Tanzanian Hadza (Apicella et al., 2014). The study found that one of the Hadza groups, whose members are familiar with market trading, exhibits an endowment effect (the group's members are unlikely to trade a lighter they have already been given for a different-colored lighter), whereas the group that is not familiar with market trading exhibits no such effect. The details, however, are revealing. Henrich warns us that the finding cannot be read as showing that the non-market-exposed Hadza are simply uncorrupted by Western culture and are therefore closer to the "natural condition" of humanity. The non-market-exposed Hadza live in their own particular cultural conditions. Henrich writes (2020, p. 389):

> It's important not to see the absence of an endowment effect among the non-market Hadza as the "natural condition" of humanity. The Hadza possess their own potent social norms, which promote the widespread sharing of food and other goods in ways not based on direct exchange, partner choice, or reciprocity. For example, they play a gambling game in which players can win each other's arrows, knives, and headbands. If chance favors a particular person and that player manages to accumulate a lot of good stuff, he is under strong social pressure to continue gambling until chance catches up with him and a degree of equality is restored. If he resists, for instance by slipping away to another camp, he'll find himself swamped with endless requests for his bounty of goods. Social norms dictate that he must share, so his store of goods won't last for more than a couple of weeks. In short, among the Hadza, one just can't get too attached to one's stuff, because soon it will be someone else's stuff. Such institutions should suppress any inclination toward an endowment effect.

The last sentence is the most revealing. Is it reasonable to describe the cultural practice outlined here, of pestering individuals who have temporarily acquired an excess of things, as working to "suppress any inclination toward an endow-ment effect"? Here, the assumption of a universal human nature manifested in individual instances seems to slide back in. Henrich's assumption seems to be that exhibiting an endowment effect is, in fact, the natural state of things, but that the particular cultural practices in the community described are preventing this effect from manifesting locally.

An alternative conclusion would be to say that to talk of an endowment effect at all in this context is simply incoherent. It is a category mistake. It is not that these non-market-trading Hadza lack an endowment effect. It is more accurate to say that the conditions in which it makes sense to talk about an endowment effect to begin with are simply not in place. The possibility of exhibiting an endowment effect – that is, the possibility of having a preference to keep what you already own in favor of something you do not yet own – presupposes a particular, Western model of ownership. If an endowment effect were a part of universal human nature, then the Western conception of personal property would also have to be part of universal human nature. This seems implausible and too Western-centric an idea for a science that claims to be universal in scope.

It might seem like researchers could solve the problem of WEIRD partici-pants by sampling more widely while translating the test materials into the local language of the test population (Broesch et al, 2020). As the Hadza example illustrates, however, this will lead to measuring non-Western populations in culturally inappropriate ways. What we end up with is not a more complete picture of human diversity, but a picture in which representations of non-Western people are distorted, using experimental materials and conceptual categories that are not appropriate for them.

What would psychological science look like without a commitment to indi-vidualism and universalism? It may be hard to imagine this, but in fact all we need to do is to look around. Alternatives abound even if they have remained at the margins of the discipline throughout its history. Here we list just a few illustrative examples.

Emphasizing the singularity of psychological phenomena as inherently local, recent work in different domains has hailed the virtues of more personalized perspectives. Research along these lines has been variously described as "idio-graphic" (Molenaar, 2004), "probatonic" (Steffensen, 2016), or "small-data" (Hekler et al., 2019), and it favors the fine-grained study of one or a few specific local cases in contrast with focusing on group averages that might not adequately capture any one individual instance. This emphasis on the unique-ness of psychological-phenomena-in-context (as opposed to the context-independence of supposedly "universal" psychological phenomena) is also in line with the "psychic pluralism" some researchers advocate as the proper theoretical starting point for psychological science (Schweder, 2015). In a different direction, but in equally varied ways, other researchers have emphasized understanding psychological phenomena at the level of entire groups, from community-based cultural approaches in developmental psychology (e.g., Rogoff, 1990, 2003) to distributed computational approaches in cognitive psychology (e.g., Hutchins, 1995). Although still in the minority, a growing number of psychologists eschew individualism and universalism, seeing culture "not as an independent variable but as the medium of human action and human life" and "cognition as situated in time and place" (Packer and Cole, 2022). This idea that psychological phenomena are situated, and can only be understood as such, has a long history and echoes themes central to the "functionalist psychology" of William James, John Dewey, and others (see, e.g., Heidbreder, 1933). Interestingly, even Wundt, a pioneer in individualistic–universalistic laboratory research, saw it as necessary for psychological science to encompass population-level and more naturalistic cultural approaches as well, which he called "Völkerpsychologie" (see, e.g., Greenwood, 2003).

As these examples make clear, there is no one way to do psychology without taking for granted individualism and universalism. What is important, for now, is to see that, as WEIRD theoretical assumptions, individualism and universalism are neither scientifically unquestionable nor absolutely necessary components of psychological science, since alternative conceptions exist. Humans are always embedded in a particular set of cultural circumstances. People are inherently culture-laden. So are the theories and tests Western psychologists have devised for asking questions about people. Solving the problem of WEIRD participants – even in the unrealistic scenario of total sampling – cannot automatically make psychological science more representative of humanity. As long as we see psychological science as in the business of seeking human universals, we will still be engaged in a Western-centric enterprise, studying phenomena carved around WEIRD boundaries and using tests that have Western assumptions baked into them.

4 WEIRD Methods

We saw in the previous section how WEIRD theoretical assumptions lead psychologists to view their own field as concerned with the universal features of thinking and behavior that are common to individuals within a population. In this section, we focus on how these theoretical assumptions shape the methods experimental psychologists use in their empirical research. We will show how WEIRD theory leads to WEIRD methods.

WEIRD methods, in short, are committed to the stimulus-response experimental approach, a useful but highly artificial and restrictive method that has survived through psychology's history. We examine the limitations inherent in the stimulus-response methodology and contrast it with less WEIRD, more naturalistic or observational approaches that have appeared at the margins of psychological science and at its border with anthropology. We will end this section by considering the possibility of "rewilding" psychological science.

4.1 The Stimulus-Response Crisis

The standard format for running a psychological experiment goes like this. First, you find a participant, who typically is naive to the purpose of the experiment. Next, you present your participant with tasks to perform and you record their behavior as they do so. Finally, you thank the participant for their time and you assure them that they will be receiving course credit in return for their participation, and then you shoo the participant out of your lab. After this is done, you will probably carry out several boring tidying-up rituals so the experimental setup is ready for the next participant. The next participant will then perform more or less the same tasks as the first. You will measure this second participant's behavior in the same way as you did with the first. You will repeat this process until you have reached what is known as adequate statistical power.

This basic format has been used in psychology laboratories ever since the origins of experimental psychology in the latter half of the nineteenth century (Danziger, 1990). The format is known as the stimulus-response paradigm. It is a useful paradigm because it allows psychologists to reliably and systematically generate new data. The stimulus-response paradigm allows psychologists to generate data that are easily comparable across different individual people. All the participants perform the same task, and their behavior is measured in the same way. This means that their behavior can be compared statistically. In principle, the stimulus-response paradigm forces experiments into a format that can be repeated, or replicated, in another psychology lab using a different set of participants.

Limitations come along with the stimulus-response paradigm. The stimulus-response experiment relies on strict experimental control of the behavior situation. In order to be able to quantify and compare the behavior of the different participants that you have sampled, you need those participants all to have performed the same task in the same way. Perhaps you show participants short videos of dogs falling off furniture, and, after each video, you ask the participant to press a button indicating how happy they feel right now. Once you have collected lots of data from different people all performing the same set of tasks, you can be fairly confident in claiming that people respond in such-and-such manner, given this particular set of stimulus materials and tasks. You might be confident in saying: "watching videos of dogs falling off furniture increases subjective well-being in a sample of Midwestern college students." Other questions immediately follow. Will people behave in the same way if you switch to slightly different stimulus materials? What happens if, say, you use videos of cats falling off furniture, or of wasps being eaten by ants? How about if you give the participants different instructions: say, after each video, instead of asking the participants how happy they feel, you ask them how confident they feel about the direction of national politics right now?

In order to answer these new questions, you will have to run a whole new set of experiments. This is fine. You can go on running new experiments in this way for a long time. What will you have learned by the end of this process – that is, by the time you have reached retirement? You will have learned a lot about how experimental participants respond to different video-and-question pairings. But How much have you learned about human psychology? How can you generalize beyond the narrow experimental paradigm you repeatedly used? How can you leverage all the data you collected in order to make conclusions about people's behavior in the real world? Realistically, the kinds of statements you will be justified in making about human nature, or human behavior in general, will be quite limited. This issue has led to the suggestion that psychology is in the midst of a generalizability crisis (Yarkoni, 2022). The suggestion is that the issue of generalizing beyond the particular experimental result is deeper than the problem of replicability and is why the replication crisis came about to begin with.

In fact, as already mentioned, the replication crisis in psychology has not affected all areas of psychology equally (Open Science Collaboration, 2015). The areas of psychology that have had the most severe troubles with replicability are precisely those areas that most heavily rely on the stimulus-response paradigm. Rather than a replication crisis or a generalizability crisis, it may be more accurate to say that psychology has for the past decade or so been undergoing a stimulus-response crisis (Wilford et al., 2022).

For our present purposes, a perhaps more important limitation of the stimulus-response paradigm is this. The paradigm is only really suitable for eliciting a certain type of behavioral response. The kinds of tasks and stimulus materials that are typically presented in the psychology lab often do not resemble behavioral situations that the average human, let us say, over the course of our evolutionary history, would ever have been likely to encounter. Nor does the psychology experiment much resemble any situation that most of us encounter in our day-to-day lives as adults. In fact, the psychology experiment most closely resembles the kinds of activities that are typically presented to children in Western educational settings. The psychology experiment, to the extent that it relies on stimulus materials that are presented and on responses that are elicited, resembles nothing so much as schoolwork. The stimulus-response style psychology experiment, in other words, is WEIRD. This is most obviously true in the case of intelligence testing.

4.2 The IQ Controversy

The idea of testing individuals in order to measure their intelligence began as a solution to a practical problem (Cole, 1996, pp. 52–53). The practical problem arose in the context of public schooling in France in the early twentieth century. The problem was that, while some children in a given class could learn efficiently, other children struggled. The educational authorities wanted a method for identifying the struggling children so they could be separated from the rest of the class and given special attention. Intelligence testing was thus developed by Alfred Binet and Theophile Simon as a means of separating schoolchildren into groups according to their aptitude.

Given that the purpose of the test was to identify children's *school aptitude*, it should be no surprise that the tasks administered as part of these early tests were the kinds of tasks a child might be expected to encounter *in school*. The tasks, arranged in order of presumed difficulty, included such things as memorizing pictures of objects, placing five weights in order, finding a word that rhymes with a given sample word, and mentally reversing the hands of a clock (Binet and Simon, 1916).

This list of tasks already includes items that would be difficult to administer to at least some non-Western populations. It should not be assumed, for example, that all languages and cultures have a concept of rhyming words. Nor do all cultures have mechanical clocks with minute and hour hands. These test items are laden with cultural knowledge specific to a particular, Western setting.

Psychologist Florence Goodenough described this problem in an address to the American Anthropological Association in 1935: "The reason that the ordinary intelligence test works as well as it does for American urban populations is simply because the items of which it is composed are fairly representative samples of the kind of intellectual tasks that American city dwellers are likely to be called upon to perform" (Goodenough, 1936). Goodenough points out that so-called tests of intelligence are wrongly understood as tools for measuring an objective property of individuals, namely their level of intelligence. Instead, intelligence tests are better understood as tools for sampling the kinds of tasks the person is likely to encounter in their daily life. Goodenough draws an analogy between the psychologist making use of intelligence testing methods to sample an individual's skills and a "thrifty housewife" checking the quality of groceries:

> The principle involved is essentially the same as that employed by the thrifty housewife who takes a handful of beans out of the barrel from which she is to purchase a supply and judges the quality of the total on the basis of this sample. ... The wise housewife, engaged in a search for a good value in beans, would not make the mistake of judging the quality of one lot on the basis of a sample taken from another lot. She would not, moreover, make the further error of assuming that the standards applied to her judgment of beans are fully valid for the judgment of potatoes. Nevertheless, errors of both these types and particularly of the latter, are all too common in much of the published work on racial [i.e., cultural] differences. (Goodenough, 1936, pp. 5–6)

Psychologists have long tried to ignore these issues by developing intelligence test methods that they claim are "culturally neutral" – that is, the testing methods do not assume any particular knowledge in the people being tested. However, the question of whether there could, even in principle, exist such culturally neutral methods remains contested. Michael Cole cites the example of Stanley Porteus, who, in the 1930s, attempted to compare intelligence across cultures using a maze game:

> Porteus carried a board with a labyrinth on it all over the world attempting to construct a hierarchy of races based on the assumption that his "maze test" was a valid, culture-free measure of general intelligence—despite the fact that among his South African samples one group that already knew a "labyrinth game" outscored all neighboring groups that did not know the game (Cole, 1996, pp. 55–56).

Arguments about the validity of comparing "intelligence" across cultural groups raged for much of the twentieth century, and indeed continue to the present (Neisser et al., 1996; Nisbett et al., 2012).

4.3 Anthropological Methods: Micronesian Navigation

One research area where the concept of intelligence has been fiercely disputed is in anthropology. This should not be surprising. Conducting successful anthropological fieldwork requires the researcher to get outside familiar modes of thinking. Anthropologists have long had to deal directly with the problems we are presently considering. In 1970, anthropologist Thomas Gladwin complained that "cognitive psychologists, like their colleagues in other areas of psychology, generally use as subjects for research and experimentation persons who are readily available and with whom they can communicate easily, which usually means college students or college graduates" (Gladwin, 1970, p. 215). It will be noted that this is simply the WEIRD participants problem, as discussed earlier. Gladwin uses this observation, however, to motivate a deeper critique of the methodological tools of cognitive science.

Gladwin is concerned, in part, with assessing the cognitive abilities of individuals from underprivileged communities in the United States. He points out that the assessment methods in use at the time that he was writing tended to treat the kinds of thinking that are typically valued within middle-class professions as the norm, from which other styles of thinking could only be seen as a deviation. He writes: "the research tools available for [quantifying this supposed deficit] are principally measurement techniques derived from concepts of intelligence developed within educational settings. Thus, rather than trying at the outset to discover qualities of thinking in underprivileged populations, researchers seek to quantify divergences from the psychological baselines used by educators, baselines rooted in middle-class intellectual culture" (Gladwin, 1970, p. 216).

To counteract the methodological bias that favors school-type testing methods, Gladwin proposed to look in detail at an unfamiliar system of thinking, one that is nevertheless demonstrably effective at dealing with the problems that arise within the cultural and geographic setting where it is used.

The system Gladwin turned to is the set of techniques used by traditional navigators who sail canoes between distantly located islands in the Caroline archipelago, which is located in Micronesia in the western Pacific. Navigators in this island system were routinely able to sail distances of up to 150 miles between islands without the aid of maps or other Western navigation tools. These navigators were "also able to tack upwind to an unseen island [located over the horizon] while keeping mental track of its changing bearing – a feat that is simply impossible for a Western navigator without instruments" (Hutchins, 1995, p. 66).

In order to understand how the Micronesian system of navigation works, it is necessary for the Western researcher to overcome a set of deeply ingrained ways of seeing the world, ways of seeing taught to them during their childhood in Western schools. Describing the Micronesian system of navigation has proved a difficult research problem for Western anthropologists, who have been working on the problem for more than a century. At the beginning of his treatment of the topic, Hutchins (1995, p. 73) writes: "The history of attempts to understand how the Micronesian navigators accomplished their way-finding feats reads like a detective story in which we know who did it but not how it was done. Each of several researchers has provided us with both useful clues and a few red herrings."

The basic problem navigators – no matter what culture they are operating in – have to solve is: where am I? To answer this, the navigator must have access to two things. What is needed is, first, a static frame of reference, and, second, at least one moving reference point that allows the navigator to keep track of the progress they have made along their course, relative to the frame of reference. The Western solution to this problem is to conceive of the geographic environment as static. In other words, the Western frame is geocentric. Maps represent the geographic environment as static and unchanging. Keeping oriented to this static environment – keeping track of where the ship currently is, in terms of the chart – is achieved with the use of tools such as a compass and an accurate clock, or, more recently, a GPS system.

Micronesian navigation culture makes use of a completely different method for keeping track of where the boat currently is. In the Micronesian system, the boat and the stars are conceived of as static while the islands are conceived of as moving. It is possible to see the stars as static, even though they move in the sky, because the stars (apart from the sun and the planets) all rise and fall at specific points of the horizon, positions that do not change throughout the year. The only exception to this, as seen from the Caroline Islands, is the North Star, or Polaris. The North Star is the star that does not move. It stays in the same position in the sky because it lies close to the imaginary line extending directly from the earth's axis of rotation. The North Star can be used as a reliable source of information for detecting where north is, while a skilled navigator can use the shape of the rest of the sky to remain oriented to the whole pattern.

With the stars seen as static, it becomes possible for the islands to move. Under normal sailing conditions, the adjacent islands are conceived of as drifting backward relative to the canoe's direction of travel (Hutchins and Hinton, 1984). One of these adjacent islands is selected as the moving point of reference for keeping track of the journey's progress. The reference island lies to the side of the boat's course, over the horizon on either the right or left side of the boat. The experienced navigator keeps track of the progress of the journey by imagining the reference island (which is not directly visible, but relative to which the navigator remains oriented) to be sliding backward along the horizon relative to the static reference frame provided by boat and stars. Micronesian navigation thus uses an allocentric frame of reference. The stars – or, more accurately, their rising and setting positions on the horizon – stay where they are, while the islands move. Describing the frame of reference in this way makes it sound exotic, but an experience of the world sliding backward relative to the observer is likely familiar to anyone who has taken a train journey through the countryside (Gladwin, 1970, p. 183).

The details of how a long canoe journey is accomplished within this allo-centric frame of reference are fascinating, and are covered in depth elsewhere (Gladwin, 1970; Hutchins, 1995). One detail from Gladwin's study is worth mentioning. When Gladwin traveled to the island where he carried out his research, he brought with him a set of Western materials for assessing cognitive abilities. One of these was a task adapted from one originally developed by Piaget. Gladwin brought six stacks of poker chips, each of a particular color. The task was to lay out pairs of poker chips so as to identify as many undupli-cated pairs as possible of contrasting colors (Gladwin, 1970, p. 228).

The poker chips Gladwin used were red, blue, white, black, yellow, and silver. The optimal solution is to start with one color and make a pair with each of the remaining colors (RB, RW, RX, RY, RS), and then repeat the process, ignoring duplicates (BW, BX, BY, BS, and so on). Only two of the participants Gladwin tested succeeded in solving this puzzle. The partici-pants who solved the puzzle were not the master navigators of the island, all of whom had been able to memorize vast amounts of information about navigation. The master navigators are held in high esteem on the island for their knowledge and skills. The two participants who successfully completed the poker chip puzzle did, however, have something else in common. They were the only two men on the island at the time who had completed their high school education, which was taken on a neighboring island (Gladwin, 1970, p. 229). Indeed, at the time of Gladwin's study, these two men were working as schoolteachers themselves (Gladwin, 1970, p. 230).

The lesson here is that, while school thinking is certainly useful, it is not the only kind of thinking that exists, and it may not be the most important kind of thinking at play in a given situation. Whole alternative systems of thinking exist outside the influence of Western schooling. To understand how such systems of thinking work, it is necessary for the researcher to go where those systems of thinking are used. We in the West are able to read about how the Micronesian system of navigation works only thanks to the hard work and humility of generations of anthropologists who put in the effort to unlearn their own ways of thinking, and – even more crucially – thanks to the cooperation of the navigators who were patient enough to teach the anthropologists something about their traditions.

4.4 Rewilding Psychology

Intelligence testing is just one area where Western ways of thinking about cognition have led to the development of psychological methods that are difficult to transfer to contexts outside of the Western educational model. It has been suggested that psychologists focus too much on "domesticated" arenas of cognition (Ibanez, 2022) – methods developed for use in formal Western institutional settings such as schoolrooms or ophthalmologists' testing rooms. Psychology's methodological tool kit has other limitations too.

Another problem is that psychologists favor the use of methodologies known to produce results in the form of statistically significant group differences. Psychologists also favor methods that can be performed over and over again. A methodology that exhibits both of these properties has obvious advantages. For one, if a study can be easily run again, then this, at least in principle, promotes the carrying out of replication studies. Given a reliable, easy-to-administer methodology, we can hope to amass a large amount of data, and to end up with a set of findings in whose truth we can have a great deal of confidence.

However, the kinds of methodologies that can be readily readministered necessarily come with some limitations. Just as the college student is the sample of convenience, so the paper survey or the computer-based response time experiment is the methodology of convenience. Some social psychologists have complained that psychology is in danger of becoming nothing more than "the science of self-reports and finger movements" (Baumeister, Vohs, and Funder, 2007). Psychology's increasing reliance on online samples and Mechanical Turk is unlikely to alleviate this problem.

If psychology is to be relevant to the study of behavior outside the laboratory, it will have to increase its methodological diversity. Newson and colleagues (2020) have suggested that the WEIRD acronym is an inadequate guide here, because it only negatively identifies the kinds of psychology we have heretofore been overemphasizing. They propose that future psychology should be more WILD, an acronym that positively identifies the kinds of questions psychologists of the future should put more effort into addressing. Future psychology should, they suggest, be Worldwide, In situ, Local, and Diverse. Newson and colleagues (2020) argue that the cognitive science of religion provides a good model. We would add that anthropological field studies, such as the Micronesian navigation case, provide another useful model for the kinds of questions toward which psychologists could turn their efforts.

Finally, we would like to draw the reader's attention to another model for conducting psychological research that requires neither the use of inherently limited laboratory techniques nor the Western-based researcher to travel to a remote part of the world. We are referring here to community-based studies of behavior as it occurs in the real world.

One of the most comprehensive attempts to understand everyday behavior by employing field research techniques was carried out by Roger Barker and his colleagues in the small town of Oskaloosa, Kansas, from the 1950s to the 1970s (Barker, 2016). Barker and colleagues' key theoretical innovation was the concept of *behavior setting*. A behavior setting is a structured unit that is larger than a single individual actor but that has discriminable boundaries in terms of time, location, participant roles, and equipment involved (Barker, 1963). Examples are a baseball game, a lecture, a group therapy session, or a single journey by canoe between two Micronesian islands.

Barker's signature insight was that if you want to predict an individual's behavior, it is often less useful to know about that individual's psychometric characteristics (such as their personality traits or their IQ score) than it is to know where they currently are. If you know that the person is in the away supporters' enclosure in a soccer stadium, then you can predict that they will behave much like everyone else in the away supporters' enclosure – for instance, you can predict that they will behave in certain ways that are characteristically different from how people in the home supporters' area are behaving, or from how the players or the snack vendors are behaving. Behavior settings theory provides a framework for applying psychological thinking to real-world behavior. The concept of behavior setting has, for instance, more recently been used to motivate research on behavior change in public health contexts (Aunger and Curtis, 2016; Curtis et al., 2019; Gautam et al., 2017). We suggest that Barker's program provides one model for how to rewild psychology, albeit one that, as Barker acknowledged, is in some ways more challenging to administer than the traditional methods of psychology (Barker, 1965).

We will return to the theme of how to make psychology less domesticated and more wild in the final section.

5 WEIRD Institutions

In the previous two sections, we considered different reasons solving the problem of WEIRD participants would not automatically make psychological science less WEIRD: merely sampling more widely, even to a far-fetched hypothetical extreme, cannot in and of itself change the fact that psychological science relies on theoretical assumptions and research methods that are not culturally neutral, but fundamentally Western-centric. This means that the problem of WEIRD participants is just one of psychology's WEIRD problems, and a relatively superficial one at that. Other, more fundamental problems make psychological science not as well suited as researchers might think for properly understanding the psychology of non-Western people, and perhaps even that of Westerners.

The current section examines ways in which, besides the specific theoretical and methodological issues we have already examined, psychological science is deeply WEIRD at the institutional level. This problem of WEIRD institutions is in some ways more fundamental than the problem of whose behavior gets studied (the problem of WEIRD participants), or the theoretical assumptions researchers take for granted (the problem of WEIRD theory) or which research methods they use (the problem of WEIRD methods). Present-day psychology is largely carried out within WEIRD institutional settings. To contribute to psychological science as it is currently structured is – usually – to participate in a fundamentally WEIRD endeavor. Experimental psychology is largely carried out within *culture-specific organizations* that rely on *culture-specific resources* to generate *culture-specific products*. In what follows, we examine each of these aspects. First, to be clear on the nature and extent of the problem, it will be helpful to approach it in light of discussions about diversity.

5.1 A Lack of Diversity among Researchers?

In Section 2 ("WEIRD Participants") we saw that psychology suffers from a lack of diversity among its participants. Psychology also suffers from lack of diversity when it comes to the researchers designing and conducting the studies.

In his analysis of APA journals, Arnett (2008) found that, overall, 73% of first authors worked at American universities (this ranged between 65% and 85% for different journals), with an additional 14% of first authors coming from other English-speaking countries and 11% from Europe, leaving only 2% for the rest of the world. In line with this, Meadon and Spurrett (2010) noted in their commentary on the original Henrich and colleagues (2010) paper: "That the subject-pool of behavioural science is so shallow is indeed a serious problem, but so is the fact that the majority of behavioural researchers are themselves deeply WEIRD" (p. 105). This matters, among other reasons, because of the close link between researcher diversity in any given dimension and the diversity of research focus and of experimental participants in that same dimension.

A good example comes from psychological research relating to race. Data on racial diversity among scientists, across disciplines, can be extremely hard to obtain, which has led to a new initiative, recently featured in *Nature*, aiming to systematically track author demographics (Else and Perkel, 2022). In the meantime, understanding the role of race in science requires piecemeal work. This is what Steven Roberts and colleagues did, examining articles published between 1974 and 2018 in top journals in cognitive, developmental, and social psychology. With regard to research focus, they found that, "across the past five decades of psychological research, few publications have highlighted the important role of race in human psychology, and virtually none have done so in cognitive psychology" (Roberts et al., 2020, p. 1298; see also Sue, 1999). Connecting research focus with researcher and participant identity, Roberts and colleagues also found that "[t]he few studies that did highlight race were written mostly by White authors, under whom there have been fewer participants of color" (p. 1303). To explain this, Roberts and colleagues suggest that "authors of color are more invested in communities of color, more cognizant of the importance of racial diversity in participant recruitment, and less likely to rely on predominantly White convenience samples" (p. 1302). To this they add, "Simply put, the research, researchers, and researched are all systematically interconnected" (pp. 1305–1306).

More generally, then, besides the well-known lack of diversity in experimental sampling that excludes non-Westerners as well as non-White, less affluent people within rich Western countries, psychology also suffers from a related lack of diversity when it comes to the researchers and the research focus: *who* conducts the research and *what* gets studied is not only a Western-centric matter, but it is also biased toward the interests of a relatively small slice of the population even within rich Western countries. So psychology does not have a single problem of lack of diversity, but many interrelated ones. As we aim to show in this section, the problem is not *only* one of lack of diversity when it comes to the individuals involved, but also, and more fundamentally, the culture-bound, distinctly WEIRD systems that give shape to contemporary psychology.

5.2 Publishing

The first institutional aspect to consider is the academic publishing system, which, at least in part, can be approached as a continuation of the preceding diversity discussion. Besides the people doing the research and the people being researched, lack of diversity is also a problem at the editorial level. Across the sciences, almost 30% of journal editors come from the United States, more than three times the second placed countries, Great Britain and Italy, each at around 7–8% (Altman and Cohen, 2021). In psychology, the numbers are even more skewed. Arnett's analysis of top APA journals showed that 100% of editors in chief were from American universities, while 82% of associate editors and editorial board members were based in the United States, the remainder coming almost entirely from other rich Western countries (Arnett, 2008). A more recent and broader analysis by Palser and colleagues found that, in the top 50 journals in psychology as ranked by citation metrics, editors were based predominantly in North America (65%) and Europe (26%) (Palser, Lazerwitz, and Fotopoulou,

2022; see also Moriguchi, 2022). As with the link between researchers and researched, there is reason to worry that lack of diversity among editors and reviewers may contribute to lack of diversity when it comes to what gets accepted for publication (see Roberts et al., 2020).

The Western-centeredness of academic publishing also goes beyond demographics at the individual level, amounting to a much larger structural issue. Academic publishing has been described as an oligopoly with just five publishers – Elsevier, Wiley, Springer, Taylor & Francis, and SAGE – responsible for more than 50% of all journal articles published in 2013 across all disciplines, 66% in the social sciences, and more than 71% of all articles in psychology alone (Larivière, Haustein, and Mongeon, 2015). Unsurprisingly, these five for-profit publishers are all rich companies based in rich Western countries: Wiley and SAGE were founded and are still headquartered in the United States; Elsevier was originally Dutch but is now owned by RELX, a publicly traded British multinational; Taylor & Francis is British and currently operates as a division of Informa, a publicly traded British group that now also owns former rival Routledge; and Springer was originally founded in Germany, but currently operates as a German–British privately held company that also owns the Nature Group as well as former Springer competitor Palgrave Macmillan.

In short, who the researchers are and where they are based, what and who they study, and who edits the journals where the research gets published are all aspects in which psychological science is Western-centric and largely demographically homogeneous; yet, independently of these points, the odds are that, for any given research project, it is one out of five publishing companies based in a rich Western country that will be in charge of making the findings public.

Why does this matter? There are many reasons, of course. A very basic one has to do with the business model these Western commercial publishing companies employ. When we say that they are in charge of turning scientific findings into public knowledge, the term "public" is more of a figure of speech: scientific articles are rarely actually publicly accessible, but are instead behind a paywall, available only through subscriptions (individual or institutional) or on a pay-per-article basis (for most readers with no academic affiliation). This makes academic publishing one of the most profitable businesses in the world (see, e.g., Larivière et al., 2015). This business model also differentially burdens researchers in developing countries, who often lack institutional access to paywalled publications (see, e.g., Simard et al., 2022). In recent years, commercial publishers have begun offering "open access" publishing options, supposedly to address this accessibility issue – however, to secure their profit margins, these options typically come with a high cost for the author's institution and are therefore less viable for authors from developing or low-income countries (see, e.g,

Kowaltowski et al., 2021). Making preprints freely available online, an increasingly common practice, addresses some of these concerns with accessibility, but it can also raise different ones, including the fear that if preprints become the end product ("no-prints") the lack of peer review could compromise the overall quality and reliability of the scientific literature (see, e.g., Mullins, 2021).

5.3 Funding

Having introduced the publishing system for disseminating research findings, the second institutional aspect to consider is the funding system that makes the research possible in the first place.

According to data from the National Science Foundation (NSF), the majority of financial support for academic research in the United States comes from the federal government, through agencies such as the National Institutes of Health (NIH), the Department of Defense (DOD), the Department of Energy (DOE), and the NSF itself, among others, which together account for more than 50% of academic research funding across fields. After the federal government, the second largest source is higher education itself, with universities providing more than 27% of the financial resources that fund academic research, followed by nonprofit organizations with 10%, the business sector with 6%, and state and local governments with more than 5% (NCSES 2022). Research in psychology corresponds to around 1.7% of the total academic research and development (R&D) costs in the United States, but the same overall pattern is at play when it comes to the distribution between the different sources: university support comes second and accounts for the same 27%, but psychologists rely more heavily on federal funds (almost 60%) and less so on funding received from all the other sources (NCSES 2021). Data from other countries are not as easily accessible, but given the United States' role and influence in contemporary psychology, the US context already provides a window into the discipline's culture-bound relationship with research funding.

Lack of diversity is a serious problem, across disciplines, when it comes to who obtains financial support to conduct research. This is very clear from recent demographic analyses of the principal investigators (PIs) receiving funding from federal agencies. Focusing on the NIH, Taffe and Gilpin (2021) found that 29% of the grants submitted by white PIs received funding, in contrast with only 17% of those submitted by African-American–Black PIs. In a similar analysis, Ginther and colleagues (2018) found that, although more experienced researchers have a higher success rate with grant applications compared to inexperienced researchers independently of race–ethnicity, a racial–ethnic gap persists at both levels, with inexperienced and experienced Black researchers always less likely to receive funding than inexperienced and experienced White researchers. As for the NSF, Chen and colleagues (2022) found that, between 1996 and 2019, the rate of success for White PIs has remained stable and above the overall rate for all submissions, with the difference below overall rates being most pronounced for Asian PIs, followed by Native Hawaiian–Pacific Islander PIs and Black–African American PIs.

Racial–ethnic disparities at the level of research funding thus further illustrates how psychology's problematic lack of diversity goes far beyond the "problem of WEIRD participants," extending to scientists within WEIRD societies. This is likely to have a compounding effect, with unequal access to funds preventing greater diversity in research focus, and culminating in the lack of diversity in published results discussed previously. Concerns with biases at the reviewing level as well as with other, more basic structural obstacles to better, more equal distribution of scientific resources have motivated debate about alternative models for allocating research funding, including even the idea of randomized, lottery-based funding for applications that cross some quality threshold (see discussions in, e.g., Avin, 2015, 2018; Bedessm, 2020; Roumbanis, 2019).

Independently of biases concerning who and what projects get funded, the question of how research is funded and by whom is of crucial importance for reflecting on psychology's institutional WEIRDness for an additional reason, namely because sources of funding can sometimes exert a non-negligible influence on scientific research and reporting. The risk is that, more than simply making it possible to conduct research, funding can also play a role in shaping the *outcomes* of the investigation. In an anonymous survey of thousands of scientists, more than 15% of respondents admitted to having "changed the design, methodology or results of a study in response to pressure from a funding source" while "12.5% admitted to overlooking others' use of flawed data" (Wadman 2005, p. 718, in reference to Martinson, Anderson, and De Vries 2005). This phenomenon has been described, especially in the biomedical and pharmacological context, as the "funding effect" (Krimsky, 2012), namely the fact that some "study outcomes were significantly different in privately funded versus publicly funded" research (p. 569), as well as when comparing results of studies funded by different commercial sponsors (see Bekelman, Li, and Gross, 2003; Lexchin et al., 2003). Although these concerns might seem most pressing when it comes to research funded by the for-profit business sector (see Holman and Elliott, 2018), the extra-scientific influence of funding sources can be worrisome in other contexts as well. Writing on a particular project in the earth sciences funded by the US military, Naomi Oreskes affirms that the researchers "did not 'paint their projects blue,' taking basic science and pretending it had military relevance. Rather, they 'painted their projects white,' cloaking military projects under the cover of basic research" (Oreskes, 2021, p. 13). In the end, this is a concern even in basic research in psychology because there is always the chance that funding sources impose biases, even if subtle ones, on the what and how of research: "whoever pays the piper calls the tune" (Tennen, 2015).

5.4 Biases and Incentives

We introduced the publishing system and the funding system as two institutional pillars that support and organize contemporary psychology. In so doing, we emphasized their Western-centric nature, the lack of diversity that characterizes them, as well as negative side effects of these WEIRD structures – in particular, the barriers for-profit companies create to accessing and publishing scientific knowledge, especially for researchers without robust funding, and the subtle as well as less subtle ways in which funding structures can compromise the reliability of published results, steering (or distorting) scientific investigation in specific directions.

These distinctly Western institutional structures central to contemporary psychology are interconnected. In a recently published article, one researcher suggests: "In psychology, doing good science (winning) means publishing a lot, placing papers in prestigious journals, having a high h-index, and securing grant money. The goal is to publish as many papers as possible by discovering as many significant findings as possible" (Haeffel, 2022, p. 2). This description casts into sharp relief the close link between funding and publishing: by financing research projects, grants provide the means for new findings and discoveries that can then be published; at the same time, having more publications, especially more highly cited ones, increases the chances of receiving funding with which to do more research and to publish more.

These intertwined systems inevitably shape how scientists think about their work and make decisions about what to investigate and how. As sociologist of science Karin Knorr-Cetina (1982, p. 110) puts it:

> Scientists talk about their "investments" in an area of research, or an experiment. They are aware of the "risks," "costs" and "returns" connected with their efforts, and talk about "selling" their results to particular journals and foundations. They seem to know which products are in high "demand," and the areas in which there is nothing to "gain." They want to put hot "products" on the "market" as quickly as possible and "earn credit" for them.

In psychology, this can lead to what Lilienfeld (2017) describes as the "corrosive impact" of psychology's "grant culture": the increasingly more common need to receive grants in order to get a job and keep it (e.g., for tenure) encourages not only blatantly questionable research practices, but also other scientifically counterproductive ones, incentivizing less risk-taking among researchers (i.e., focusing on more easily fundable projects), as well as promoting greater intellectual hyperspecialization (i.e., focusing on the same set of related ideas or problems for several years or decades). The grant culture can also invert the usual logic of research, turning grants from a means into an end, and making grant applications the researcher's equivalent of the hamster's wheel (Lilienfeld, 2017).

These systemic problems relating to funding are inseparable from publishing biases. One example is the widely acknowledged bias in the psychological literature toward positive findings. The rate of success reported by psychologists has been described as unrealistic, too good to be true, leading to the conclusion that this cannot be because all psychological theories are correct, but instead because only significant findings are being reported (Bakker, Van Dijk, and Wicherts, 2012; Haeffel, 2022). This lack of transparency becomes a systemic problem as it is sustained at the editing–reviewing level: editors and peer reviewers typically judge more favorably papers that report statistically significant findings, and this in turn encourages researchers to prioritize reporting studies that have positive findings and perhaps only those, which ultimately makes it impossible for the scientific community to know which hypothesis have failed to be supported, which findings have not been replicated, which studies got shelved because no conclusive result was obtained, and so on (Bakker et al., 2012).

Related to this bias toward reporting only positive findings is the bias in *how* the findings get reported. Recent textual analysis by Jasmine DeJesus and colleagues revealed that, in 11 journals from different subfields in psychology, 89% of the articles contained at least one generic formulation of the research finding. These generic claims – such as "introverts and extraverts require different learning environments" or "animal, but not human, faces engage the distributed face network in adolescents with autism" – misleadingly frame the finding as a timeless universal fact (rather than the result of a specific measurement that it is), hiding all diversity and exceptions that may hold (DeJesus et al., 2019, p. 18370). This bias toward bold, flashy claims is perpetuated by academic publishers and popular media alike, and it gets in the way of accurate knowledge dissemination and understanding of scientific findings. Important for the present discussion, this bias is not itself universal, but depends on the population sampled: when the psychological research draws predominantly from White US participants, the findings are more likely to be framed as general universal facts; in contrast, when based on non-White US participants as well as non-Western populations, findings tend to include reference to ethnicity or geographical markers, suggesting that these findings are seen as potentially more local and limited in scope compared to the evidence obtained from White US samples (Cheon, Melani, and Hong, 2020; DeJesus et al., 2019). As others have observed, "Authors studying non-WEIRD samples are often asked to justify why they chose to study a particular group" (Klein, Savaş, and Conley, 2022, p. 815), which reveals "biases among reviewers and editors about the 'generalizability' of findings from WEIRD contexts" (p. 814).

To conclude, psychology unquestionably suffers from a lack of diversity when it comes to demographics at the individual level, including the researchers, the researched, the editors and publishers, the funders and the funded; but far beyond the individuals involved, and beyond even their theoretical and methodological commitments, psychology is WEIRD at the institutional level, in the way that psychological research is structured, from beginning to end. As we have seen, the current publishing and funding systems hamper access to scientific knowledge (especially for non-Westerners) and also hamper access to opportunities to do research (for many researchers even within WEIRD societies). Worse, these systems can also be scientifically counterproductive: influencing what gets investigated and how, disproportionately favoring positive findings, and encouraging the misrepresentation of those findings in a Western-centric universalistic way can lead to poorer understanding of psychological phenomena everywhere, in Western and non-Western contexts alike.

6 UnWEIRDing Psychology?

In the previous sections, we identified multiple interrelated ways in which contemporary psychological science is culture-bound and Western-centric. Our starting point, in Section 2, was the widely acknowledged problem that the typical participants in psychological experiments – college students in the United States – cannot reasonably be considered neutral representatives of humanity as a whole. This problem, which we called the "problem of WEIRD participants," has received much attention over the past decade, but it is only one of psychology's WEIRD problems. Moving gradually from this well-known problem, we have shown how research in psychological science is built upon WEIRD theoretical assumptions (Section 3) and it applies WEIRD methods (Section 4), all supported and shaped by WEIRD institutional struc-tures (Section 5). This means that the widely acknowledged problem of WEIRD participants, although serious, is the most superficial of psychology's WEIRD problems: even if we could solve it by sampling much more widely, the other problems would still exist because the science itself, in its current form, is deeply culture-bound and Western-centric.

In fact, as we have suggested, both the *problem* of WEIRD participants and the *motivation for solving it* can be seen as symptomatic of psychological science's WEIRDness. On the one hand, the problem of WEIRD participants arises because of how psychology is practiced and structured: WEIRD institutional biases and incentives (e.g., in publishing and funding) encourage scientists to use experimental methods of convenience (methods that are limited and WEIRD, e.g., stimulus-response, self-report paradigms) to study mind and behavior by sampling participants of convenience (predominantly WEIRD college students), with WEIRD theoretical assumptions about mind and behavior in relation to individuals and species as well as in relation to nature and culture (i.e., scientific individualism and scientific universalism) being used, even if implicitly, to justify the use of samples and methods of convenience (e.g. treating individuals as windows to "universal human nature"). On the other hand, the same WEIRD theoretical assumptions have over the past decade been invoked to motivate countering the current methodological and institutional limitations so as to diversify the participant pool and solve the problem of WEIRD participants (i.e., so we can have an even more accurate picture of "universal human nature"). This means that, besides being more fundamental than – and even causing – the problem of WEIRD participants, psychology's WEIRD theoretical, methodological, and institutional problems are also intertwined with each other, making it difficult to tackle any one of these problems (as well as properly addressing the problem of WEIRD participants) in complete isolation from the other problems (see Figure 3).

The question that remains is whether and how this multiply problematic situation can be addressed. The theoretical, methodological, and institutional problems we have examined are "basic" or "foundational" in that they concern the basis or foundations upon which the edifice of contemporary psychology has been built. Accordingly, they raise a question about the extent of required renovations and whether the building can be improved upon pretty much as it stands, or whether more radical reconstruction is called for. Could our multiply WEIRD psychological science be unWEIRDed?

6.1 Beyond Helicopters and Parachutes

Over the past decade, and across fields and disciplines, there has been growing criticism of what is variously described as "helicopter research" or "parachute science": these are brief research trips, often in Africa or Asia, in which researchers from rich Western countries fly in, collect the data they need, and then fly out to conduct the analysis and interpretation back at home, all with minimal (if any) involvement from and direct benefit to local researchers or the

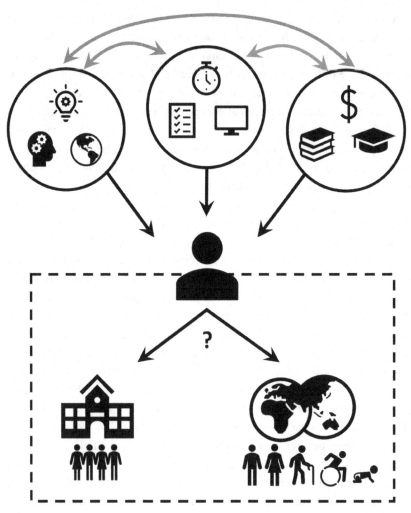

Figure 3 Elaborating on Figure 2, here we emphasize the interconnection of psychology's WEIRD problems (gray bidirectional arrows at the top). WEIRD theoretical assumptions, in particular individualist and universalist ideas about mind and behavior (top left), go hand in hand with WEIRD experimental methods of sampling individual responses in statistically comparable ways (top middle). WEIRD institutional biases and incentives (top right) are shaped by dominant theoretical and methodological commitments, and they also reinforce these by influencing what research gets funded and published. Whose behavior *is* studied (dashed box) is itself a product of these WEIRD theoretical, methodological and institutional problems: merely solving the problem of WEIRD participants by sampling more widely is insufficient to address psychology's other WEIRD theoretical, methodological, and institutional

local population. This approach to international research has been criticized as ethnocentric and colonialist, perpetuating power and privilege imbalances that "present a scientific, ethical and moral threat to psychological science" (Singh, 2022, p. 272; see also, e.g., Adams, Osei-Tutu, and Affram, 2020; Crookes and Warren, 2022; Haelewaters, Hofmann, and Romero-Olivares, 2021; Minasny et al., 2020; Wada and Suzuki, 2019).

Despite this recent flood of publications condemning helicopter research, it is worth noting that neither the practice nor the criticism are new. An early example of helicopter research was the 1898 Cambridge anthropological expedition to the Torres Strait between Australia and Papua New Guinea. Expedition members investigated a number of different topics, including "kinship relations, languages, color categorization, rituals, and indigenous music" (Costall, 1999, p. 345). The expedition's organizer later described these as laying the foundations of "ethnical [*sic*] experimental psychology," moving beyond readily accessible participants who were "mainly Europeans or of European descent" so as to, "for the first time," investigate "by means of an adequate laboratory equipment a people in a low stage of culture under their ordinary conditions of life" (Haddon and Quiggin, 1910, pp. 103–104). The expedition's problematic legacy has been explored in detail elsewhere (see, e.g., Herle and Rouse, 1998; Richards, 1997, 1998). Importantly, the psychological results reported were also heavily criticized early on, including by E. B. Titchener, who commented in detail on the tests used, which he considered "inadequate to their purpose" (Titchener, 1916, p. 204), among other reasons, because of translation errors due to cross-culturally inappropriate assumptions about color categories (on this see also, e.g., Kusch, 2014).

Long before the current concern with helicopter research, the same types of practices under different names had already been denounced and alternatives proposed. One suggestive label used from the 1960s through the 1980s was "safari research," described as "a quick sojourn by the western investigator to bag the data with the help of local labour, which he then drags home for analysis, ultimately mounting his prize in some publication for admiration by other safari hunters" (Bochner, 1969, p. 158). This description by Stephen Bochner comes

---

Caption for Figure 3 (cont.)

problems; at the same time, however, the question of whose behavior *should be* studied, as well as which behavior and how (question mark in the middle), can only be properly addressed in light of reflection on those other, more fundamental theoretical, methodological, and institutional problems.

from a report about a workshop held in the summer of 1968 to promote collaborations between researchers from Australia and the United States with international colleagues representing seven countries in Asia (India, Philippines, South Korea, Japan, Samoa, Sri Lanka, Thailand). On the challenges attending cross-cultural research, Bochner, himself a workshop participant, noted that "[p]roblems or concepts which may be meaningful in one culture need not be so in another, or may have a totally different meaning," such that "a study which reports data collected in more than one country is not truly cross-cultural unless the investigation has been jointly planned, designed and carried out by research workers from both cultures" (Bochner, 1969, pp. 158–159). In line with this and related observations, the workshop organizer, F. Kenneth Berrien, proposed the following recommendations for properly conducting international research:

> The best cross-cultural research is that which: (1) engages the collaborative efforts of two or more investigators of different countries, each of whom is (2) strongly encouraged and supported by institutions in their respective countries to (3) address researchable problems of a common concern not only to the science of psychology but (4) relevant to the social problems of our times. Such collaborative enterprises would begin with (5) the joint definition of the problems, (6) employ comparable methods, (7) pool data that would be "owned" by the collaborators jointly who are free to (8) report their own interpretations to their own constituents but (9) are obligated to strive for interpretations acceptable to a world community of scholars. (Berrien, 1970, pp. 33–34)

These recommendations are similar, in terms of breadth and depth, to other more recently proposed improvements on helicopter research (see, e.g., the "ten rules" proposed by Haelewaters et al., 2021). This suggests the contemporary challenge, as well as proposed remedies, to be recapitulations of old lessons not learned.

Given our focus in this Element, it is useful to situate these criticisms of helicopter (or parachute, or safari) research in relation to the WEIRD problems we identified in the previous sections.

Strictly speaking, helicopter research is a solution to the problem of WEIRD participants. That is, given the widespread recognition that contemporary psychological science is overly reliant on college students in the United States and that Western researchers would do well to sample behavior much more widely across cultures, then it would seem that actually going "out there" and collecting more data from more varied sources is precisely what needs to be done. The fact that so many scientists find helicopter research questionable can, we think, be interpreted as implicit acknowledgment that the problem of WEIRD participants is the least of psychology's WEIRD problems: the reason this approach to sampling more widely is inadequate is that it "solves" the sampling problem without addressing the more fundamental ways in which psychology is theoretically, methodologically, and institutionally culture-bound and Western-centric.

In fact, not only is helicopter research a poor way to solve the problem of WEIRD participants (on this there is wide agreement in the literature), but it can only be considered a solution at all *because of* theoretical, methodological, and institutional biases like the ones we identified in the previous sections. That is, helicopter research can only *seem* to be minimally acceptable if you take for granted the theoretical assumptions of individualism and universalism, and if you operate under the methodological assumption of the stimulus-response paradigm: only if you operate under these assumptions at home (e.g., in the United States) could it seem reasonable to show up in remote areas in Africa or Asia, recruit individual participants, expose them to artificial experimental stimuli imported from a different context, and record their responses as a step to learning about universal, psychological human nature. Accepting these WEIRD theoretical and methodological assumptions all the while ignoring psychology's Western-centric and culture-bound institutional dimension makes it possible to see helicopter research as something that could be improved, but that is not fundamentally misguided. In contrast, however, acknowledging these WEIRD assumptions and structures motivates remaining vigilant even in true close collaborations with non-Western researchers: after all, for Western researchers looking for potential collaborators in non-Western contexts whom they consider well-trained, "being a well-trained researcher can mean [having] a well-westernized mind" (Azuma, 1981, p. 25), and, accordingly, having "the very blinders that contemporary psychologists seek to remove" through the collaboration (Cole, 2006, p. 913). Helicopter research is a bad way to solve psychology's WEIRD problems because it targets only the sampling problem. What is more, depending on who the collaborators are, even careful cross-cultural projects might not be enough to fully circumvent the WEIRD theoretical, methodological, and institutional limitations characteristic of contemporary psychology.

To be clear, these points go far beyond the domain of international psychological research, but concern the discipline as a whole. In the cross-cultural context, although Western research typically aims to find out the extent to which Western theories apply to non-Western groups, some psychologists have recently suggested that work in the opposite direction is also necessary: "psychology should generalize from – not just to – Africa" (Adetula et al., 2022; see also, e.g., Holdstock, 2013). Helicopter research cannot, however, be seen as a problem only when it comes to Western researchers studying populations abroad. The same types of practices are common and can also be highly problematic even within WEIRD countries, such as in research on so-called diverse populations targeting non-White, low-income, or otherwise minoritized participants. In these cases, even the most well-meaning scientist would struggle to do good science if they simply parachute from the ivory tower bringing in their own biases and preconceptions, without greater involvement from the population studied (see, e.g., Haelewaters et al., 2021; Rowley and Camacho, 2015). This parallel between international and local research suggests that progress in both might require greater public participation in science: just as with cross-cultural collaboration, maybe it is always the case that science is best done only when the populations studied are deeply involved in the research from beginning to end (see, e.g., Dunlap et al., 2021; Evans and Potochnik, forthcoming; Santana, 2022; Schroeder, 2022). In line with this, greater attention to scholarship emerging from different contexts outside the Western mainstream – including, but not limited to, indigenous and decolonial perspectives, such as in Latin American liberation psychology – could not only enhance Western *cross-cultural* research, but even lead to more fundamental transformation when it comes to the theoretical, methodological, and institutional dimensions of psychological science as practiced *within* the Western context (see, e.g., Adams et al., 2015; Adams et al., 2019; Forscher et al., 2021; Gergen et al., 1996; IJzerman et al., 2021; Silan et al., 2021).

6.2 Should Psychology Be Narrow or Wide?

In this Element, we have been discussing a collection of crises scientific psychology has faced over the past decade or so. These crises have generally been treated as distinct from one another, although overlapping. Each crisis has been given its own name. We have mentioned the crisis of replicability (Pashler and Wagenmakers, 2012), the crisis of generalizability (Yarkoni, 2022), and the crisis of unrepresentative subject samples – that is, the WEIRD participants problem (Henrich et al., 2010; see Section 2). We could have mentioned others, such as the crisis in cumulative theoretical progress (Muthukrishna, Henrich, and Slingerland, 2021).

It seems reasonable to ask: why has psychological science been experiencing so many crises simultaneously? We might wonder whether it is really appropriate to talk of multiple crises at all. Perhaps these crises are not distinct from one another, but manifestations of a single, underlying systemic failure.

The evidence we have discussed suggests an answer to what that systemic failure might be. There is a contradiction at the heart of modern scientific psychology. The field's overall goal is ambitious, but the tools for pursuing this goal are too limited. The field aims to derive universal, truthful conclusions about humanity in general, but it aims to do so by means of the null-hypothesis-based laboratory experiment, which is a powerful tool for generating knowledge, but it allows researchers to ask questions only in a restricted format suspiciously reminiscent of activity that takes place in Western schooling and other "domesticated" contexts (Ibanez, 2022).

To resolve this contradiction, scientific psychology has a choice to make. It can choose between two main options. First, it could choose to go narrow. That is, it could restrict its ambitions. It could restrict itself to asking narrow-format questions suited to the tools available in existing psychology laboratories. There are advantages to this approach. For one, this approach is consistent with how psychology is already run. The price of taking this approach is that psychologists must accept that the science they are pursuing is not a science of *Homo sapiens*. Instead, it is a culture-specific study of educated Western minds under the social and economic conditions that prevail in Western societies. The study of non-Western behavior sits awkwardly within this narrow purview.

Alternatively, scientific psychology could choose to go wide. It could choose to expand its toolbox so as to enable the pursuit of a broader range of research questions than psychologists have traditionally been able to ask. This second alternative was the rallying cry of Henrich and colleagues' original WEIRD paper (Henrich et al., 2010). These authors suggested that psychology needs to broaden its participant pool. We have seen, however, that merely broadening the participant pool will not be sufficient to lead to a psychology that can adequately investigate human behavior and mental life in all its variety. Expanding our existing, WEIRD-centric psychology into a truly inclusive science of human thinking and behavior will require flexibility. It will require flexibility in both theoretical assumptions and methodological commitments, and, above all, it will require cooperation from the populations being investigated.

6.3 Going Ecological

Laboratory-based experimentation will always have an important place within psychology. The development of laboratory methods can reasonably be said to mark the beginning of modern psychology as a discipline (Danziger, 1990). For as long as psychologists continue to use laboratory methods, there will always be questions about the extent to which those experiments' results are relevant to life beyond the laboratory walls. This question is often discussed in terms of "ecological validity" – a term with a somewhat confused history (Araujo, Davids, and Passos, 2007).

Concerns about the extent to which traditional laboratory methods can adequately capture the behavioral phenomenon of interest are ubiquitous in experimental psychology. They arise even within fields of psychology engaged with basic processes such as visual perception. In the introduction to his final book, psychologist of perception James J. Gibson wrote:

> The great virtue of the headrest, the bite-board, the exposure device, the tachistoscope, the darkroom with its points of light, and the laboratory with its carefully drawn pictorial stimuli was that they made it possible to study vision experimentally. The only way to be sure an observer sees what he says he does is to set up an experimental situation and check him out. Experimental verification can be trusted. These controls, however, made it seem as if snapshot vision and aperture vision were the whole of it, or at least the only vision that could be studied. But, on the contrary, natural vision can be studied experimentally. . . . It is not true that "the laboratory can never be like life." The laboratory must be like life! (Gibson, 1979, p. 3)

Gibson's signature insight was that some types of visual information only become available to the individual if you allow them to move. Forward movement creates a pattern of optic flow on the observer's retinas, expanding centrifugally from the place where the observer is heading (Koenderink, 1986). To the classical laboratory-based psychophysicist, this optic flow is unwelcome visual noise that makes it difficult to isolate an experimental variable of interest.

Gibson realized, however, that for an individual animal, the optic flow pattern is crucial. The flow pattern is what allows the individual to perceive where they are heading and to control their movement, to decide when to stop walking forward so as to avoid colliding into things (Gibson, 1958). Gibson realized, in other words, that the tools of the ophthalmologist are useful and have their place, but they are too restrictive, too narrow, to capture the living phenomenon of visual perception as it exists in the real world. Perception, considered as a phenomenon at the scale of behavioral ecology, is fundamentally about movement – precisely the thing psychophysicists had rendered impossible in their pursuit of experimental control.

To suggest that psychology can overcome its WEIRD problems by abandoning its laboratory tools would be too simplistic. Psychology's WEIRD problems will always be present because they are necessarily baked into the methodological and theoretical assumptions that make it possible to run experiments in the first place. Assumptions are necessary in science. Psychology can no more do without making at least some assumptions than it can do without the concept of measurement.

The lesson of the WEIRD debate, and of psychology's decade of crisis in general, is that scientific psychology must maintain an attitude of constant vigilance. Our theoretical commitments, methodological tools, and institutional arrangements all tend to pressure individual scientists into adopting an instrumental, formulaic attitude to knowledge production. Our tools threaten to not only constrain but to dictate the kinds of questions we are allowed to ask. The generation of statistically significant findings threatens to become psychology's only goal, at the cost of the pursuit of other meaningful questions.

Henrich and colleagues' (2010) original paper suggested that the psychology of the future must be more diverse and it must investigate participants from every possible cultural background. We agree with this in principle. It would be nice if every experiment could be run simultaneously at multiple locations around the world. There are, however, considerable practical barriers to such an arrangement. Not least problematic are the political questions involved. For example, who gets to decide which research questions should be prioritized?

We therefore do not offer any panacea for psychology's WEIRD problems. Indeed, we are tempted to conclude that psychology will enter its post-WEIRD age only when Western research institutions are no longer the primary producers of psychological knowledge.

One positive conclusion can be drawn, however. It is that laboratory research should be seen as a tool for confirming hypotheses, not as an end in itself. Laboratory methods should be seen as a supplement to the study of behavior in the world, not be mistaken for the actual object of interest. Being ecological does not require the researcher to coordinate data collection at a dozen different sites around the world (although doing so can of course be a worthwhile project). It requires only that effort is taken to ensure that laboratory-based research questions are tied to real behavior with a real-world, wild counterpart. Psychologists should always be wary of getting hung up on aspects of behavior that are merely artifacts of the domesticated setting of the laboratory (Ibanez, 2022).

In addition to quantitative, experimental methods, psychology once embraced qualitative methods, including case reports and field studies. "The conventional methodological wisdom of [this earlier] era," according to Sears, "was that the researcher must travel back and forth between field and laboratory (and their differing indigenous populations) in order to bracket properly any sociopsychological phenomenon" (Sears, 1986, p. 516). These earlier psychologists demonstrated a sensible attitude. We have much to learn from the psychologists of the past.

References

Adams, G., Dobles, I., Gómez, L. H., Kurtiş, T. & Molina, L. E. (2015). Decolonizing psychological science: Introduction to the special thematic section. *Journal of Social and Political Psychology*, 3(1), 213–238.

Adams, G., Estrada-Villalta, S., Sullivan, D. & Markus, H. R. (2019). The psychology of neoliberalism and the neoliberalism of psychology. *Journal of Social Issues*, 75(1), 189–216.

Adams, G., Osei-Tutu, A. & Affram, A. A. (2020). Decolonial perspectives on psychology and development. In *Oxford Research Encyclopedia of Psychology*. Oxford University Press.

Adetula, A., Forscher, P. S., Basnight-Brown, D., Azouaghe, S., & IJzerman, H. (2022). Psychology should generalize from – not just to – Africa. *Nature Reviews Psychology*, 1(7), 370–371.

Adolph, K. E. (2019). An ecological approach to learning in (not and) development. *Human Development*, 63(3–4), 180–201.

Altman, M. & Cohen, P. N. (2021). Openness and diversity in journal editorial boards. https://doi.org/10.31235/osf.io/4nq97.

Apicella, C. L., Azevedo, E. M., Christakis, N. A. & Fowler, J. H. (2014). Evolutionary origins of the endowment effect: Evidence from hunter-gatherers. *American Economic Review*, 104(6), 1793–1805. https://doi.org/10.1257/aer.104.6.1793.

Apicella, C., Norenzayan, A. & Henrich, J. (2020). Beyond WEIRD: A review of the last decade and a look ahead to the global laboratory of the future. *Evolution and Human Behavior*, 41(5), 319–329.

Araujo, D., Davids, K. & Passos, P. (2007). Ecological validity, representative design, and correspondence between experimental task constraints and behavioral setting: Comment on Rogers, Kadar, and Costall (2005). *Ecological Psychology*, 19(1), 69–78.

Arechar, A. A. & Rand, D. G. (2021). Turking in the time of COVID. *Behavior Research Methods*, 53(6), 2591–2595.

Arnett, J. J. (2008). The neglected 95%: Why American psychology needs to become less American. *American Psychologist*, 63(7), 602–614.

Aunger, R. & Curtis, V. (2016). Behaviour centred design: Towards an applied science of behaviour change. *Health Psychology Review*, 10(4), 425–446.

Avin, S. (2015). Funding science by lottery. In Mäki, U., Votsis, I., Ruphy, S. & Schurz, G. editors., *Recent Developments in the Philosophy of Science: EPSA13 Helsinki* (pp. 111–126). Springer.

Avin, S. (2018). Policy considerations for random allocation of research funds. *RT: A Journal on Research Policy and Evaluation*, 6(1), 1–27.

Azuma, H. (1981). A note on cross-cultural study. *Quarterly Newsletter of the Laboratory of Comparative Human Cognition*, 3(2), 23–25.

Baggs, E., Raja, V. & Anderson, M. L. (2019). Culture in the world shapes culture in the head (and vice versa). *Behavioral and Brain Sciences*, 42 (e172), 16–17.

Baggs, E., Raja, V. & Anderson, M. L. (2020). Extended skill learning. *Frontiers in Psychology*, 11(1956). https://www/doi.org/10.3389/fpsyg.2020.01956.

Bakker, M., Van Dijk, A. & Wicherts, J. M. (2012). The rules of the game called psychological science. *Perspectives on Psychological Science*, 7(6), 543–554.

Barker, J. S. (2016). Why 25 years? Notes on the long trajectory of Roger Barker's research in Oskaloosa. *Ecological Psychology*, 28(1), 39–55.

Barker, R. G. (1963). On the nature of the environment. *Journal of Social Issues*, 19(4), 17–38.

Barker, R. G. (1965). Explorations in ecological psychology. *American Psychologist*, 20(1), 1–14.

Barrett, H. C. (2020). Towards a cognitive science of the human: Cross-cultural approaches and their urgency. *Trends in Cognitive Sciences*, 24(8), 620–638.

Baumeister, R. F., Vohs, K. D. & Funder, D. C. (2007). Psychology as the science of self-reports and finger movements: Whatever happened to actual behavior? *Perspectives on Psychological Science*, 2(4), 396–403.

Beckelman, J. E., Li, Y. & Gross, C. P. (2003). Scope and impact of financial conflicts of interest in biomedical research. *Journal of the American Medical Association*, 289, 454–465.

Bedessem, B. (2020). Should we fund research randomly? An epistemological criticism of the lottery model as an alternative to peer review for the funding of science. *Research Evaluation*, 29(2), 150–157.

Berlin, B. (1992). *Ethnobiological Classification: Principles of Categorization of Plants and Animals in Traditional Societies*. Princeton University Press.

Bernhard, H., Fischbacher, U. & Fehr, E. (2006). Parochial altruism in humans. *Nature*, 442(7105), 912–915.

Berrien, F. K. (1970). A super-ego for cross-cultural research. *International Journal of Psychology*, 5(1), 33–39.

Binet, A. & Simon, T. (1916). New methods for the diagnosis of the intellectual level of subnormals. In Goddard, H. H., editor, *The Development of Intelligence in Children* (pp. 37–90). Williams & Wilkins.

Bochner, S. (1969). The Honolulu workshop-conference on psychological problems in changing societies. *Australian Psychologist*, 3(3), 158–162.

Broesch, T., Crittenden, A. N., Beheim, B. A. et al. (2020). Navigating cross-cultural research: Methodological and ethical considerations. *Proceedings of the Royal Society B*, 287(1935), 20201245.

Buhrmester, M., Kwang, T. & Gosling, S. D. (2011). Amazon's Mechanical Turk: A new source of inexpensive, yet high-quality, data? *Perspectives on Psychological Science*, 6(1), 3–5.

Chen, C. Y., Kahanamoku, S. S., Tripati, A. et al. (2022). Decades of systemic racial disparities in funding rates at the National Science Foundation. eLife 11:e83071 https://doi.org/10.7554/eLife.83071.

Cheon, B. K., Melani, I. & Hong, Y. Y. (2020). How USA-centric is psychology? An archival study of implicit assumptions of generalizability of findings to human nature based on origins of study samples. *Social Psychological and Personality Science*, 11(7), 928–937.

Christie, R. (1965). Some implications of research trends in social psychology. In Klineberg, O. & Christie, R., editors, *Perspectives in Social Psychology* (pp. 141–152). Holt, Rinehart & Winston.

Choi, J. K. & Bowles, S. (2007). The coevolution of parochial altruism and war. *Science*, 318(5850), 636–640.

Cohen, J. (1994). The earth is round (p < .05). *American Psychologist*, 49(12), 997–1003.

Cole, M. (1996). *Cultural Psychology: A Once and Future Discipline*. Harvard University Press.

Cole, M. (2006). Internationalism in psychology: We need it now more than ever. *American Psychologist*, 61(8), 904–917.

Costall, A. (1999). Dire straits: The divisive legacy of the 1898 Cambridge anthropological expedition. *Journal of the History of the Behavioral Sciences*, 35(4), 345–358.

Crookes, A. E. & Warren, M. A. (2022). Authorship and building psychological research in low and middle income countries: A view from the Pacific island nation of Fiji. *South African Journal of Psychology*, 52(2), 154–160.

Curtis, V., Dreibelbis, R., Buxton, H. et al. (2019). Behaviour settings theory applied to domestic water use in Nigeria: A new conceptual tool for the study of routine behaviour. *Social Science & Medicine*, 235, 112398.

Danziger, K. (1990). *Constructing the Subject: Historical Origins of Psychological Research*. Cambridge University Press.

Danziger, K. (1997). *Naming the Mind: How Psychology Found Its Language*. Sage.

DeJesus, J. M., Callanan, M. A., Solis, G. & Gelman, S. A. (2019). Generic language in scientific communication. *Proceedings of the National Academy of Sciences*, 116(37), 18370–18377.

Dunlap, L., Corris, A., Jacquart, M., Biener, Z. & Potochnik, A. (2021). Divergence of values and goals in participatory research. *Studies in History and Philosophy of Science Part A*, 88, 284–291.

Earp, B. D. & Trafimow, D. (2015). Replication, falsification, and the crisis of confidence in social psychology. *Frontiers in Psychology*, 6, 621. https://doi .org/10.3389/fpsyg.2015.00621.

Else, H. & Perkel, J. M. (2022). The giant plan to track diversity in research journals. *Nature*, 602(7898), 566–570.

Evans, A. & Potochnik, A. (forthcoming). Theorizing participatory research. In Anderson, E., editor, *Ethical Issues in Stakeholder-Engaged Health Research*. Springer.

Forscher, P. S., Basnight-Brown, D. M., Dutra, N. et al. (2021). Psychological science needs the entire globe: Part 3. *APS Observer*, 35.

Fort, K., Adda, G. & Cohen, K. B. (2011). Amazon Mechanical Turk: Gold mine or coal mine? *Computational Linguistics*, 37(2), 413–420.

Flynn, J. R. (2007). *What Is Intelligence? Beyond the Flynn Effect*. Cambridge University Press.

Gallander Wintre, M., North, C. & Sugar, L. A. (2001). Psychologists' response to criticisms about research based on undergraduate participants: A developmental perspective. *Canadian Psychology*, 42(3), 216–225.

Gautam, O. P., Schmidt, W.-P., Cairncross, S., Cavill, S. & Curtis, V. (2017). Trial of a novel intervention to improve multiple food hygiene behaviors in Nepal. *American Journal of Tropical Medicine and Hygiene*, 96(6), 1415–1426.

Gergen, K. J., Gulerce, A., Lock, A. & Misra, G. (1996). Psychological science in cultural context. *American Psychologist*, 51(5), 496–503.

Gibson, J. J. (1958). Visually controlled locomotion and visual orientation in animals. *British Journal of Psychology*, 49(3), 182–194.

Gibson, J. J. (1979). *The Ecological Approach to Visual Perception*. Houghton-Mifflin.

Ginther, D. K., Basner, J., Jensen, U. et al. (2018). Publications as predictors of racial and ethnic differences in NIH research awards. *PLoS One*, 13(11), e0205929.

Gladwin, T. (1970). *East Is a Big Bird: Navigation and Logic on Puluwat Atoll*. Harvard University Press.

Gleibs, I. H. & Albayrak-Aydemir, N. (2022). Ethical concerns arising from recruiting workers from Amazon's Mechanical Turk as research participants:

Commentary on Burnette et al. (2021). *International Journal of Eating Disorders*, 55(2), 276–277.

Goodenough, F. L. (1936). The measurement of mental functions in primitive groups. *American Anthropologist*, 38(1), 1–11.

Goodman, J. K. & Wright, S. (2022). MTurk and online panel research: The impact of COVID-19, bots, TikTok, and other contemporary developments. In Lamberton, C., Rucker, D., and Spiller, S. A., editors, *The Cambridge Handbook of Consumer Psychology.* 2nd edition. Cambridge University Press.

Graham, S. (1992). "Most of the subjects were white and middle class": Trends in published research on African Americans in selected APA journals, 1970–1989. *American Psychologist*, 47(5), 629–639.

Greenwood, J. D. (2003). *The Disappearance of the Social in American Social Psychology.* Cambridge University Press.

Haddon, A. C. & Quiggin, A. H. (1910). *History of Anthropology.* Putnam.

Haelewaters, D., Hofmann, T. A. & Romero-Olivares, A. L. (2021). Ten simple rules for Global North researchers to stop perpetuating helicopter research in the Global South. *PLoS Computational Biology*, 17(8), e1009277.

Haeffel, G. J. (2022). Psychology needs to get tired of winning. *Royal Society Open Science*, 9(6), 220099.

Harré, R. (1984). *Personal Being: A Theory for Individual Psychology.* Harvard University Press.

Heath, J. (2020). Methodological Individualism. *Stanford Encyclopedia of Philosophy* (Summer 2020 Edition), Edward N. Zalta (ed.). https://plato.stanford.edu/archives/sum2020/entries/methodological-individualism.

Heidbreder E. (1933). *Seven Psychologies.* Appleton-Century-Crofts.

Hekler, E. B., Klasnja, P., Chevance, G. et al. (2019). Why we need a small data paradigm. *BMC Medicine*, 17(1), 1–9.

Henrich, J. (2015). *The Secret of Our Success: How Culture Is Driving Human Evolution, Domesticating Our Species, and Making Us Smarter.* Princeton University Press.

Henrich, J. (2020). *The WEIRDest People in the World: How the West Became Psychologically Peculiar and Particularly Prosperous.* Penguin UK.

Henrich, J., Ensminger, J., McElreath, R. et al. (2010). Markets, religion, community size, and the evolution of fairness and punishment. *Science*, 327(5972), 1480–1484.

Henrich, J., Heine, S. J. & Norenzayan, A. (2010). The weirdest people in the world? *Behavioral and Brain Sciences*, 33(2–3), 61–83.

Herle, A., & Rouse, S. (Eds.). (1998). *Cambridge and the Torres Strait: Centenary Essays on the 1898 Anthropological Expedition*. Cambridge University Press.

Herrmann, B., Thoni, C. & Gachter, S. (2008). Antisocial punishment across societies. *Science*, 319(5868), 1362–1367.

Higbee, K. L., Lott, W. J. & Graves, J. P. (1976). Experimentation and college students in social psychology research. *Personality and Social Psychology Bulletin*, 2(3), 239–241.

Higbee, K. L., Millard, R. J. & Folkman, J. R. (1982). Social psychology research during the 1970s: Predominance of experimentation and college students. *Personality and Social Psychology Bulletin*, 8(1), 180–183.

Higbee, K. L. & Wells, M. G. (1972). Some research trends in social psychology during the 1960s. *American Psychologist*, 27(10), 963–966.

Holdstock, L. T. (2013). *Re-examining Psychology: Critical Perspectives and African Insights*. Routledge.

Holman, B. & Elliott, K. C. (2018). The promise and perils of industry-funded science. *Philosophy Compass*, 13(11), e12544.

Hruschka, D. J. & Henrich, J. (2013). Economic and evolutionary hypotheses for cross-population variation in parochialism. *Frontiers in Human Neuroscience*, 7, 559. https://doi.org/10.3389/fnhum.2013.00559.

Hruschka, D. J., Medin, D. L., Rogoff, B. & Henrich, J. (2018). Pressing questions in the study of psychological and behavioral diversity. *Proceedings of the National Academy of Sciences*, 115(45), 11366–11368.

Hutchins, E. (1995). *Cognition in the Wild*. MIT Press.

Hutchins, E. & Hinton, G. E. (1984). Why the islands move. *Perception*, 13(5), 629–632.

Ibanez, A. (2022). The mind's golden cage and cognition in the wild. *Trends in Cognitive Sciences*, 26(12), 1031–1034.

IJzerman, H., Dutra, N., Silan, M. et al. (2021). Psychological science needs the entire globe. *APS Observer*, 34(5). https://www.psychologicalscience.org/observer/global-psych-science.

Ioannidis, J. P. A. (2005). Why most published research findings are false. *PLoS Medicine*, 2(8):e124.

Kahneman, D., Knetsch, J. L. & Thaler, R. H. (1990). Experimental tests of the endowment effect and the Coase theorem. *Journal of Political Economy*, 98 (6), 1325–1348.

Keller, E. F. (2010). *The Mirage of a Space between Nature and Nurture*. Duke University Press.

Kidwell, M. C., Lazarevíc, L. B., Baranski, E. et al. (2016). Badges to acknowledge open practices: A simple, low-cost, effective method for increasing transparency. *PLoS Biology*, 14(5), e1002456.

Klein, R. A., Ratliff, K. A., Vianello, M. et al. (2014). Investigating variation in replicability: A "many labs" replication project. *Social Psychology*, 45(3), 142. Preprint: https://osf.io/wx7ck.

Klein, V., Savaş, Ö. & Conley, T. D. (2022). How WEIRD and androcentric is sex research? Global inequities in study populations. *Journal of Sex Research*, 59(7), 810–817.

Knorr-Cetina, K. D. (1982). Scientific communities or transepistemic arenas of research? A critique of quasi-economic models of science. *Social Studies of Science*, 12(1), 101–130.

Koenderink, J. J. (1986). Optic flow. *Vision Research*, 26(1), 161–179.

Kowaltowski, A. J., Oliveira, M., Silber, A. & Chaimovich, H. (2021). The push for open access is making science less inclusive. *Times Higher Education.* http://bit.ly/3mgOJ1X.

Krimsky, S. (2012). Do financial conflicts of interest bias research? An inquiry into the "funding effect" hypothesis. *Science, Technology, & Human Values*, 38(4), 566–587.

Kusch, M. (2014). Wittgenstein as a commentator on the psychology and anthropology of colour. In Gierlinger, F. & Riegelnik, S., editors, *Wittgenstein on Colour* (pp. 93–107). Walter de Gruyter.

Laland, K., Brown, G., Hannon, E. & Lewens, T. (2018). The social construction of human nature. In Hannon, E. & Lewens, T., editors, *Why We Disagree about Human Nature* (pp. 127–144). Oxford University Press.

Laland, K., Matthews, B. & Feldman, M. W. (2016). An introduction to niche construction theory. *Evolutionary Ecology*, 30(2), 191–202.

Lang, M., Purzycki, B. G., Apicella, C. L. et al. (2019). Moralizing gods, impartiality and religious parochialism across 15 societies. *Proceedings of the Royal Society B: Biological Sciences*, 286, 1–10.

Larivière, V., Haustein, S. & Mongeon, P. (2015). The oligopoly of academic publishers in the digital era. *PloS One*, 10(6), e0127502.

Levinson, S. C., Kita, S., Haun, D. B. M. & Rasch, B. H. (2002). Returning the tables: Language affects spatial reasoning. *Cognition*, 84(2), 155–188.

Lewontin, R. C. (1983). The organism as the subject and object of evolution. *Scientia*, 118(1–8), 65–95

Lewontin, R. C. (2001). *The Triple Helix: Gene, Organism, and Environment.* Harvard University Press.

Lexchin, J., Bero, L. A., Djulbegovic, B. & Clark, O. (2003). Pharmaceutical industry sponsorship and research outcome and quality: Systematic review. *British Medical Journal*, 326, 1167–1170.

Li, P. & Gleitman, L. (2002). Turning the tables: Language and spatial reasoning. *Cognition*, 83(3), 265–294.

Lilienfeld, S. O. (2017). Psychology's replication crisis and the grant culture: Righting the ship. *Perspectives on Psychological Science*, 12(4), 660–664.

Litman, L., & Robinson, J. (2020). *Conducting Online Research on Amazon Mechanical Turk and Beyond*. Sage.

Makel, M. C., Plucker, J. A. & Hegarty, B. (2012). Replications in psychology research: How often do they really occur? *Perspectives on Psychological Science*, 7(6), 537–542.

Martinson, B. C., Anderson, M. S. & De Vries, R. (2005). Scientists behaving badly. *Nature*, 435(7043), 737–738.

McNemar, Q. (1946). Opinion-attitude methodology. *Psychological Bulletin*, 43(4), 289–374.

Meadon, M. & Spurrett, D. (2010). It's not just the subjects: There are too many WEIRD researchers. *Behavioral and Brain Sciences*, 33(2–3), 104–105.

Medin, D. L. & Atran, S. (2004). The native mind: Biological categorization and reasoning in development and across cultures. *Psychological Review*, 111 (4), 960–983.

Minasny, B., Fiantis, D., Mulyanto, B., Sulaeman, Y. & Widyatmanti, W. (2020). Global soil science research collaboration in the 21st century: Time to end helicopter research. *Geoderma*, 373, 114299.

Molenaar, P. C. (2004). A manifesto on psychology as idiographic science: Bringing the person back into scientific psychology, this time forever. *Measurement*, 2(4), 201–218.

Moriguchi, Y. (2022). Beyond bias to Western participants, authors, and editors in developmental science. *Infant and Child Development*, 31(1), e2256.

Moss, A. J., Rosenzweig, C., Robinson, J., Jaffe, S. N. & Litman, L. (2020a). Is it ethical to use Mechanical Turk for behavioral research? Relevant data from a representative survey of MTurk participants and wages. https://doi.org/10.31234/osf.io/jbc9d.

Moss, A. J., Rosenzweig, C., Robinson, J. & Litman, L. (2020b). Demographic stability on Mechanical Turk despite COVID-19. *Trends in Cognitive Sciences*, 24(9), 678–680.

Mullins, M. (2021). Opinion: The problem with preprints. *The Scientist*. http://bit.ly/3J2ouFK.

Muthukrishna, M., Henrich, J. & Slingerland, E. (2021). Psychology as a historical science. *Annual Review of Psychology*, 72, 717–749.

National Center for Science and Engineering Statistics (NCSES) (2022). *National Patterns of R&D Resources: 2019–20 Data Update*. NSF 22–320. National Science Foundation. https://ncses.nsf.gov/pubs/nsf22320.

National Center for Science and Engineering Statistics (NCSES) (2021). *Higher Education Research and Development: Fiscal Year 2020.* NSF 22–311. National Science Foundation. https://ncses.nsf.gov/pubs/nsf22311.

Neisser, U., Boodoo, G., Bouchard, T. J. et al. (1996). Intelligence: Knowns and Unknowns. *American Psychologist,* 51(2), 77–101.

Newson, M., Buhrmester, M., Xygalatas, D. & Whitehouse, H. (2020). Go WILD, not WEIRD. *Journal for the Cognitive Science of Religion,* 6(1–2), 80–106.

Nisbett, R. E., Aronson, J., Blair, C. et al. (2012). Intelligence: New findings and theoretical developments. *American Psychologist,* 67(2), 130–159.

Norenzayan, A., Choi, I. & Peng, K. (2007). Perception and cognition. In Kitayama, S. & Cohen, D., editors, *Handbook of Cultural Psychology* (pp. 569–594). Guilford Press.

Norenzayan, A., Shariff, A. F., Gervais, W. M. et al. (2016). Parochial prosocial religions: Historical and contemporary evidence for a cultural evolutionary process. *Behavioral and Brain Sciences,* 39, E29.

Nosek, B. A., Hardwicke, T. E., Moshontz, H. et al. (2022). Replicability, robustness, and reproducibility in psychological science. *Annual Review of Psychology,* 73, 719–748.

Odling-Smee, F. J. (1988). Niche constructing phenotypes. In Plotkin, H. C., editor, *The Role of Behavior in Evolution* (pp. 73–132). MIT Press

Odling-Smee, J., Erwin, D. H., Palkovacs, E. P., Feldman, M. W. & Laland, K. N. (2013). Niche construction theory: A practical guide for ecologists. *Quarterly Review of Biology,* 88(1), 3–28.

Open Science Collaboration (2015). Estimating the reproducibility of psychological science. *Science,* 349(6251), aac4716.

Oreskes, N. (2021). *Science on a Mission: How Military Funding Shaped What We Do and Don't Know about the Ocean.* University of Chicago Press.

Oyama, S. (1985/2000). *The Ontogeny of Information: Developmental Systems and Evolution.* Duke University Press.

Oyama, S., Gray, R. D. & Griffiths, P. E. (Eds.). (2003). *Cycles of Contingency: Developmental Systems and Evolution.* MIT Press.

Packer, M. J. & Cole, M. (2022). The challenges to the study of cultural variation in cognition. *Review of Philosophy and Psychology,* 1–23.

Palser, E. R., Lazerwitz, M. & Fotopoulou, A. (2022). Gender and geographical disparity in editorial boards of journals in psychology and neuroscience. *Nature Neuroscience,* 25(3), 272–279.

Paolacci, G. & Chandler, J. (2014). Inside the Turk: Understanding Mechanical Turk as a participant pool. *Current Directions in Psychological Science,* 23(3), 184–188.

Parke, R. D. (2000). Beyond white and middle class: Cultural variations in families – assessments, processes, and policies. *Journal of Family Psychology*, 14(3), 331–333.

Pashler, H. & Wagenmakers, E.-J. (2012). Editors' introduction to the special section on replicability in psychological science: A crisis of confidence? *Perspectives on Psychological Science*, 7(6), 528–530.

Peterson, R. A. (2001). On the use of college students in social science research: Insights from a second-order meta-analysis. *Journal of Consumer Research*, 28(3), 450–461.

Richards, G. (1997). *"Race," Racism and Psychology*. Routledge.

Richards, G. (1998). Getting a result: The expedition's psychological research 1898–1913. In Herle, A. & Rouse, S., editors, *Cambridge and the Torres Strait: Centenary Essays on the 1898 Anthropological Expedition* (pp. 136–157). Cambridge University Press.

Roberts, S. O., Bareket-Shavit, C., Dollins, F. A., Goldie, P. D. & Mortenson, E. (2020). Racial inequality in psychological research: Trends of the past and recommendations for the future. *Perspectives on Psychological Science*, 15(6), 1295–1309.

Rogoff, B. (1990). *Apprenticeship in Thinking: Cognitive Development in Social Context*. Oxford University Press.

Rogoff, B. (2003). *The Cultural Nature of Human Development*. Oxford University Press.

Roumbanis, L. (2019). Peer review or lottery? A critical analysis of two different forms of decision-making mechanisms for allocation of research grants. *Science, Technology, & Human Values*, 44(6), 994–1019.

Rowley, S. J. & Camacho, T. C. (2015). Increasing diversity in cognitive developmental research: Issues and solutions. *Journal of Cognition and Development*, 16(5), 683–692.

Salari Rad, M., Martingano, A. J. & Ginges, J. (2018). Toward a psychology of *Homo sapiens*: Making psychological science more representative of the human population. *Proceedings of the National Academy of Sciences*, 115 (45), 11401–11405.

Santana, C. (2022). Why citizen review might beat peer review at identifying pursuitworthy scientific research. *Studies in History and Philosophy of Science*, 92, 20–26.

Schimmack, U. (2020). A meta-psychological perspective on the decade of replication failures in social psychology. *Canadian Psychology/ Psychologie canadienne*, 61(4), 364–376. https://doi.org/10.1037/cap00 00246.

Schroeder, S. A. (2022). Diversifying science: Comparing the benefits of citizen science with the benefits of bringing more women into science. *Synthese*, 200(4), 1–20.

Sears, D. O. (1986). College sophomores in the laboratory: Influences of a narrow data base on social psychology's view of human nature. *Journal of Personality and Social Psychology*, 51(3), 515–530.

Segall, M. H., Campbell, D. T. & Herskovits, M. J. (1966). *The Influence of Culture on Visual Perception*. Bobbs-Merrill.

Shank, D. B. (2016). Using crowdsourcing websites for sociological research: The case of Amazon Mechanical Turk. *American Sociologist*, 47(1), 47–55.

Shrout, P. E. & Rodgers, J. L. (2018). Psychology, science, and knowledge construction: Broadening perspectives from the replication crisis. *Annual Review of Psychology*, 69(1), 487–510.

Shweder, R. A. (2015). Cultural psychology. In Wright, J., editor, *International Encyclopedia of the Social & Behavioral Sciences (Second Edition)* (pp. 478–483). Elsevier.

Shweder, R. A., Much, N. C., Mahapatra, M. & Park, L. (1997). The "big three" of morality (autonomy, community, divinity) and the "big three" explanations of suffering. In Rozin, A. M. B. P., editor, *Morality and Health* (pp. 119–169). Routledge.

Silan, M., Adetula, A., Basnight-Brown, D. M. et al. (2021). Psychological science needs the entire globe, part 2. *APS Observer*, 34(6).

Simard, M. A., Ghiasi, G., Mongeon, P. & Larivière, V. (2022). National differences in dissemination and use of open access literature. *PloS One*, 17(8), e0272730.

Simmons, J. P., Nelson, L. D. & Simonsohn, U. (2011). False-positive psychology: Undisclosed flexibility in data collection and analysis allows presenting anything as significant. *Psychological Science*, 22(11), 1359–1366.

Simons, D. J., Shoda, Y. & Lindsay, D. S. (2017). Constraints on generality (COG): A proposed addition to all empirical papers. *Perspectives on Psychological Science*, 12(6), 1123–1128.

Singh, L. (2022). Navigating equity and justice in international collaborations. *Nature Reviews Psychology*, 1, 372–373. https://doi.org/10.1038/s44159-022-00077-5.

Smart, R. G. (1966). Subject selection bias in psychological research. *Canadian Psychologist*, 7a(2), 115–121.

Steffensen, S. V. (2016). Cognitive probatonics: Towards an ecological psychology of cognitive particulars. *New Ideas in Psychology*, 42, 29–38.

Stotz, K. & Griffiths, P. (2018). A developmental systems account of human nature. In Hannon, E. & Lewens, T., editors, *Why We Disagree about Human Nature* (pp. 58–75). Oxford University Press.

Sue, S. (1999). Science, ethnicity, and bias: Where have we gone wrong? *American Psychologist*, 54(12), 1070–1077.

Tackett, J. L., Brandes, C. M., King, K. M., & Markon, K. E. (2019). Psychology's replication crisis and clinical psychological science. *Annual Review of Clinical Psychology*, 15, 579–604.

Tackett, J. L., Lilienfeld, S. O., Patrick, C. J. et al. (2017). It's time to broaden the replicability conversation: Thoughts for and from clinical psychological science. *Perspectives on Psychological Science*, 12(5), 742–756.

Taffe, M. A. & Gilpin, N. W. (2021). Equity, diversity and inclusion: Racial inequity in grant funding from the US National Institutes of Health. *eLife*, 10, e65697.

Taylor, C. (1989). *Sources of the Self: The Making of the Modern Identity*. Harvard University Press.

Tennen, H. (2015). Whoever pays the piper calls the tune: A case of documenting funding sources. In Sternberg, R. J. & Fiske, S. T. editors, *Ethical Challenges in the Behavioral and Brain Sciences* (pp. 208–2011). Cambridge University Press.

Thalmayer, A. G., Toscanelli, C. & Arnett, J. J. (2021). The neglected 95% revisited: Is American psychology becoming less American? *American Psychologist*, 76(1), 115–132.

Titchener, E. B. (1916). On ethnological tests of sensation and perception with special reference to tests of color vision and tactile discrimination described in the reports of the Cambridge anthropological expedition to Torres Straits. *Proceedings of the American Philosophical Society*, 55(3), 204–236.

Wada, K. & Suzuki, H. (2019). "All other things being equal": Conducting crosscultural research in counselling psychology. *Proceedings from the 2018 Canadian Counselling Psychology Conference*, 162–175. http://hdl.handle.net/1880/111418.

Wadman, M. (2005). One in three scientists confesses to having sinned. *Nature*, 435(7043), 718–720.

Weber, M. (1922). *Economy and Society*, 2 volumes. G. Roth and C. Wittich (eds.), University of California Press, 1968.

Webster Jr, M. (1973). Psychological reductionism, methodological individualism, and large-scale problems. *American Sociological Review*, 38(2), 258–273.

Wilford, R., Ardila-Cifuentes, J., Baggs, E. & Anderson, M. L. (2022). The stimulus-response crisis. *Behavioral and Brain Sciences*, 45(e39), 70–72.

Williamson, V. (2016). On the ethics of crowdsourced research. *PS: Political Science & Politics*, 49(1), 77–81.

Yarkoni, T. (2022). The generalizability crisis. *Behavioral and Brain Sciences*, 45(e1), 1–78.

Yong, E. (2012). Replication studies: Bad copy. *Nature*, 485(7398), 298–300.

Acknowledgements

We acknowledge support by the Open Access Publication Fund of the Technical University of Berlin.

Psychology and Culture

Kenneth D. Keith

University of San Diego

Kenneth D. Keith is author or editor of more than 160 publications on cross-cultural psychology, quality of life, intellectual disability, and the teaching of psychology. He was the 2017 president of the Society for the Teaching of Psychology.

About the Series

Elements in Psychology and Culture features authoritative surveys and updates on key topics in cultural, cross-cultural, and indigenous psychology. Authors are internationally recognized scholars whose work is at the forefront of their subdisciplines within the realm of psychology and culture.

Cambridge Elements ≡

Psychology and Culture

Elements in the Series

A full series listing is available at: www.cambridge.org/EPAC

Printed in the United States
by Baker & Taylor Publisher Services